Pearls of Wisdom

"Again, the kingdom of heaven is like a merchant looking for fine pearls."
Matthew 13:45

Dr. C.

clfpublishing.org
909.315.3161

Cover design by Senir Design. Contact info: info@senirdesign.com

ISBN #978-1-945102-87-5

Printed in the United States of America.

Dedication

To every person who has ever thought about how life can be better, more peaceful, and more joyful.

Acknowledgements

Thank you Heavenly Father for your wisdom you have poured out upon me, so I may share it with others. I'm grateful and honored. Bless your Holy Name!

Table of Contents

Peace

It does not mean to be

in a place where there

is no noise, trouble,

or hard work. It means

to be in the midst of

those things and still be

calm in your heart.

You Took My Parking Space at Church

One day, a man went to visit a church. He got there early, parked his car, and got out. Another car pulled up near the car, the driver got out and said, "I always park there! You took my place!"
The visitor went inside for Sunday school, found an empty seat, and sat down. A young lady from the church approached him and stated, "That's my seat! You took my place!" The visitor was somewhat distressed by this rude welcome, but he said nothing.

After Sunday school, the visitor went into the sanctuary and sat down. Another member walked up to him and said, "That's where I always sit! You took my place!" The visitor was even more troubled by this treatment, but still he said nothing.

Later as the congregation was praying for Christ to dwell among them, the visitor stood up and His appearance began to change. Horrible scars became visible on His hands and on His sandaled feet. Someone from the congregation noticed Him and called out, "What happened to you?" The visitor replied, as his hat became a crown of thorns and a teal tear fell down from His eye,
"I took your place."

After reading this, say a prayer. That's all you have to do. This is powerful. Maybe, just maybe, we can get the world to start thinking of who took our place.

Sometimes you may
feel God is hard on you
and doesn't love you. The
truth is He loves you too
much to leave
you the
way you are.

Pearl #1
Think Before You Speak or Act

When a child is harassed by a bully who spouts insults and expletives, a popular phrase to respond with is, "Sticks and stones may break my bones, but words will never hurt me." And, the child who utters those words does so with the hope that the words will render truth in his/her life even though times have undoubtedly proved differently. By the time the child reaches adulthood, he/she has learned that merely speaking the words of the popular phrase does not make them true.

From our own experiences with other people, we under-stand words *can* be hurtful. Sometimes, the damage we have sustained or inflicted upon others is far worse than that of sticks and stones. However, even with this truth, we still speak without considering the impact our words will have in a person's life.

In a moment's notice, we have at times flown off the handle without stopping to think about the consequences of what we are about to say. Other times, we react to something someone said or did and start attacking that person with cruel accusations or vicious threats. The damage of our words could be so profound, and the damage could forever sever a personal relationship we have with a person or cause a lasting strain. Flying off the handle without stopping to think about the repercussions will lead to people getting hurt, and later, people will be sorry for what they said. But, unfortunately, the damage will be done.

Author Yehuda Berg states, "Words are singularly the most powerful force available to humanity. Words have energy and power with the ability to help, to heal, to hurt, to harm, to humiliate and to humble." Berg's perspective is corroborated by James 3:8-12 (NIV), which informs us, *"No human being can tame the tongue. It is a restless evil, full of deadly poison. With the tongue we praise our Lord and Father, and with it we curse human beings, who have been made in God's likeness. Out of the same mouth come praise and cursing. My brothers and sisters, this should not be. Can both fresh water and salt water flow from the same spring? My brothers and sisters, can a fig tree bear olives, or a grapevine bear figs? Neither can a salt spring produce fresh water."*

The words we choose and how we choose to use them can build others up or tear them down; they can bring a community together or rip it apart; they can breed joy or discontentment. For as the Bible says, *"Death and life are in the power of the tongue"* (Proverbs 18:21, KJV). What is your objective when you speak? To build or to tear down?

Choose the words you will speak very carefully because they have the potential of accomplishing nearly anything or destroying nearly anything. Just one negative comment can ruin a person's day. A few might even ruin the person's life. On the flip side, one positive and encouraging comment can be just enough to increase personal engagement, create healthier cultures and make more of a difference in an individual's life than you will ever know. Our words are powerful and should be treated with respect.

Let's examine how our words impact others and how we can choose them wisely to eliminate heartache and suffering and instead germinate life, encouragement, peace, and hope.

Words are powerful!

One of the greatest mistakes we can make is believing our words have no impact or weight in other people's lives. Within the words we speak is an emotional potency. Each word we use can have a colossal impact. Never think of words as inconsequential. Instead, think of them as powerful. Words can build up or tear down. They can motivate or discourage. They can empower or weaken.

Even if people pretend to ignore our words (and they often do), can they actually unhear what we say? Of course not! People do not suddenly become deaf when we begin to speak. And no matter if they tell us our opinion is of no consequence or our perspective is a nonfactor, they still hear us when we speak.

Put yourself in their position for just a moment. Recall a heated conversation you had with someone. Can you still remember the person's words practically verbatim even years down the road? Now consider a similar conversation in someone else's life. Your words could be the ones *he/she* has in *his/her* head. Why is that? Because words sting, and they have lasting impressions. Most importantly, once words are spoken, they cannot be unspoken nor can they be unheard! No matter how much the speaker or the hearer may want that to be true.

The words we choose mean something. Whether that meaning is positive or negative is up to you. If you want to live positively and make a positive, healthy impact in the world, try starting with the daily words you choose. How do you talk to others, to yourself, to your superiors, and to your inferiors? When we recognize the value our words have, we take the first step in bettering our community, our workplaces, our homes, our temperaments, and our dispositions by disarming ourselves of words that breed hatred, discontentment, anger, strife, bitterness, jealousy, and envy. Again, life and death are in the power of your tongue (Proverbs 18:21). Render life unto those with whom you come in contact by thinking before you speak.

Words are remembered.

If words have meaning, then they are definitely remembered. Consider the child in class whose teacher tells him he's never going to be as good of a student as his older sister. This comment, which could mean nothing to the teacher, will always be remembered by the child and viewed as a statement of disappointment. Unknowingly, the child could inadvertently decide not to try to improve his scholastic skillset and/or the child could begin to resent his older sister.

In contrast, think of the child whose teacher tells him how much she believes in him. Even a simple comment can forever make an impact to either uplift or defeat. To live a positive and impactful life is to recognize our words are not just for today. Even though they may be spoken today, they will continue to live on every day after today. What you say today could be remembered for years to come, so choose your words carefully. The best way to do that is to stop and think before you speak. Be mindful of those who will hear your words. Consider how the words will impact them.

Words make a difference.

Words... are... powerful! Think of powerful words throughout history which have made a lasting difference in our world. *"Four score and seven years ago." "I have a dream." "Tear down this wall."* Our words, when chosen correctly, can make a positive contribution in our own lives and the lives of those around us.

Words filter through us and seep into our community, where they are absorbed then reasserted by others to people they know. When we recognize the power our words have, we see the impact they can have and we choose them based on what kind of difference we want to make. Furthermore, by choosing our words carefully in front of our youth can save generations to come by depositing positivity instead of negativity and words that divide, conquer, defeat, separate, spurn, isolate, degrade, debilitate, and maim.

Speak with mindfulness.

How can we choose our words wisely? First, we should know whether the words have a negative or positive connotation. Second, based on the usage of the words, we can use them or find a more suitable word for the circumstance. Mindfulness is more than just thinking before speaking.

It's recognizing the people around us and promoting a more compassionate society through our language choice. Also, think about the image you project to others. What image do you want your name to embody? One of positivity, love, and compassion or one of degradation and despair? Do you want people to sit and hear what you have to say, or do you want them to leave the room before you enter because they are not interested in what you have to say?

If you elect to embody a positive image and breathe life into others, rather than speaking out emotionally and uncontrollably on any issue, give careful consideration and thought to how your words could impact others. It means recognizing poor language choice and readjusting to live a more loving life. The way you speak -- the attitude and tone -- reflects the person you are and impacts everything around you. It can greatly contribute to your success or "non-success" both in business and your personal life. So next time, think before you speak. It will make all the difference.

The words you choose in your life have *meaning*. They will be *remembered*. They make a *difference*. When we recognize the power our words have, we can harness that power to be a force for good, and possibly a force of change, in the community around us. Matt Mayberry (former Chicago Bears linebacker) says, "Speak every word you say in life as though it were your last."

After considering your words, if you find them to be lacking in benefit, you may reason that it might be best to not say anything at all. I was always told that if you can't say something nice, don't say anything at all. As Benjamin Franklin once said,

"Remember not only to say the right thing in the right place, but far more difficult still, to leave unsaid the wrong thing at the tempting moment."

One final helpful tip: to reduce the use of harmful words, refer to Galatians 5:22-23, which provide nine fruit we should have in our lives: *"But the fruit of the Spirit is love, joy, peace, longsuffering, gentleness, goodness, faith, meekness, temperance: against such there is no law."* Increase your faith in God by reading His Word and watch the fruit of the Spirit be added into your life. Having them will prove to be a great asset in changing the words you use on a daily basis.

Just as it is very important to think before we speak, it is equally important to think before we act. If we perform an action that is not well thought out, we could cause harm to ourselves and others; we could commit an act whose damage is irreversible; and we could even commit an act that is life threatening or illegal. To prevent unnecessary harm to others and/or ourselves, it is best to exercise restraint within our ourselves by giving thought before moving into action.

Below, there are fifteen points that can guide you in making the right decision about which action (if any) is appropriate for each given situation.

1. Gain the correct perspective.
Before attempting to make a decision about how to respond in a given situation, make sure you have the correct perspective of the situation at hand. Doing so will allow you to step back in an

effort to see the bigger picture rather than what may prove to be a limited perspective. Any misinterpretation of the situation will lead to the wrong response. Never assume you know why an action occurred. Your assumption about someone else's reasoning can quickly lead you to an inappropriate response. Knowledge is key. Assumptions lead to miscalculations and misled and misdirected responses.

2. Use empathy.

Empathy is the ability to imagine how someone else feels in a given situation, allowing yourself an opportunity to momentarily step into the person's place. If you are able to understand his/her point of view, you may gain more information about the situation and be able to make better decisions based on that perspective. Avoid assuming the other person is wrong or misguided, as this will not allow you to gain his/her perspective.

3. Make sure your facts are correct.

Obtaining factual information that will serve as your premise is vital. Operating with non-factual information will lead to an ill-drawn conclusion, which could in turn lead to an unwarranted action. Having the facts will help minimize any potential misperceptions you could have about the situation. Verifying the facts before you act will help ensure you do not have a misconception about what has occurred. Misperceptions can increase the likelihood of conflict, which does decrease the likelihood of cooperation.

4. Take time to listen to others.

In order to gain the perspective of others, you must first listen and understand their needs and how they are feeling. Then, when you have listened and understood their concern, then you can respond and offer advice. After all, how can advice be given if you have not listened or fully comprehended a person's concern? Oftentimes, people are so full of 'wisdom' that they cannot wait to share it. But is it really wise to offer advice without listening to the whole matter? Listening to the entire matter takes patience. Patience to listen, not only to hear. Patience to comprehend by giving the person's words some thought. And, patience to provide sound advice.

5. Consider the person's perspective.

When you make assumptions about another person's words or intentions, you are likely to make a snap judgement, especially in a situation that is already heated. Try to avoid these judgments by trying to see things from someone else's perspective. This will decrease conflict that may create unhelpful tense situations.

6. Consider the possible outcomes.

Considering possible outcomes of your actions is important because you can be blinded by your emotions, which can lead you to acting impulsively. By considering what could happen, this can help you prevent impulsive or rash decisions. With rational thoughts, the best outcomes will result. Irrational thoughts, on the other hand, will lead to destruction, hurt feelings, disappointment, etc.

7. Know which emotions to use.

Emotions are important because they help you make decisions by providing feedback on the situations you are in. However, you must know which emotions to use and when. If you ignore the emotions of others or if you try to suppress them, they can lead to tension, which will create conflict.

8. Your feelings are real.

When you think about how your emotions affect you and your decisions, you must realize that your reactions are real. In other words, it is important to realize that others will feel the same way as you do. You can use this to your advantage by showing empathy and understanding their point of view.

9. This is not about you.

You must realize that other people's reactions are not always going to be beneficial to you. When you understand this concept, it will help you recognize that there are other issues at play and you are not necessarily the focal point.

10. Learn from the past.

Everyone has had a negative experience with another person. When this happens, we must learn from it and take steps to ensure it does not happen again. Think about how you will make sure the same thing doesn't happen again. This can help you create and maintain a healthy relationship for both parties involved, which is a possible outcome.

11. Look for your mistakes.

If you only focus on the negative impacts others have created within a situation, you will create a tense atmosphere. However, when you look at a situation openly and honestly, you can see the mistakes you are making. Then, you can more accurately think about how you can improve your behavior rather than focus on those of others. By not doing this, you will only have a negative view of others and place blame on them when it could be yours to own.

12. Accept the feelings of others.

If you believe your feelings are valid, you should give the same courtesy and respect to others for their feelings. You may not like their feelings, but it is an individual's right to experience whatever feelings dwell inside of him/her. You should refrain from telling others how to feel or how not to feel. Doing so can incite an unwanted response, which could in turn lead to an unwanted reaction.

13. Respond with a question to give you time.

Responding with a question is a great way to avoid doing something you might regret later down the line. This way, you can get your point across while being able to take the time to think about your response.

14. Recognize the difference between right and wrong.

If we cannot tell the difference between right and wrong, then we are more likely to make a mistake. By recognizing this, we can become more aware that our actions will have consequences and they may be unwanted or undesired consequences. By doing this, you will be able to recognize the issues that are causing tension.

15. Don't try and change other people.
It's also important to understand you cannot force others to change. Instead of trying to change them, work with them so a solution that is going to benefit everyone involved can be found.

Reacting negatively rather than responding positively and respectfully will undoubtedly create tension in our relationships with other people. By learning how to respond rather than react, we will be able to create healthier relationships across the board. If we recognize our words or response is going to cause toxic tension, then we can save ourselves from making a mistake and from giving others heartache. It is also important to realize that this doesn't mean we will be happy about what happens next. However, by learning to understand others, we can create an environment where everyone feels valued and respected. This will not only help us feel as representatives of God but also make sure there are no misunderstandings between us and others. This will create a benefit for everyone involved and therefore create a healthy relationship.

WHEN YOU TRUST GOD TO
FULFILL THE PROMISES HE'S
GIVEN YOU, ALL THE FORCES
OF DARKNESS CANNOT STOP
GOD FROM BRINGING YOUR
DREAMS TO PASS.

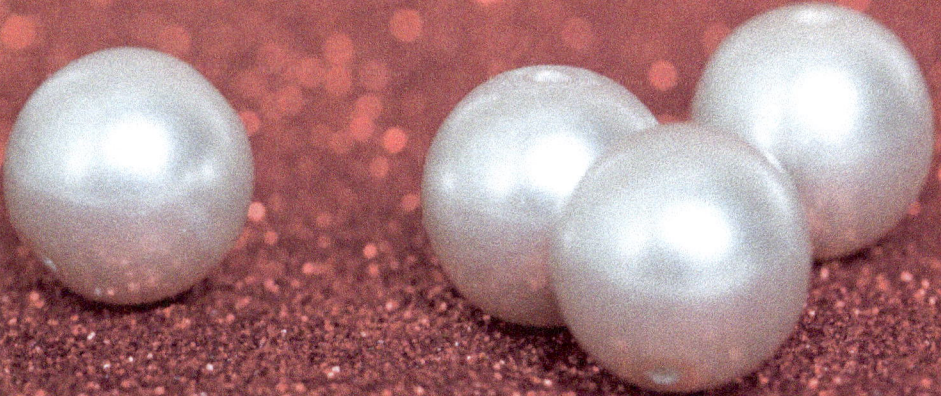

"Yes, you are a wonderful companion, but you are not perfect. Sometimes, the problem is YOU."

Pensacola Helene

Love is patient and kind.

Love is not jealous or boastful or

proud or rude.

It does not demand its own way.

It is not irritable, and it keeps no

record of being wronged.

It does not rejoice about injustice but

rejoices whenever the truth wins out.

Love never gives up, never loses faith,

is always hopeful, and endures

through every circumstance.

I Corinthians 13:4-7

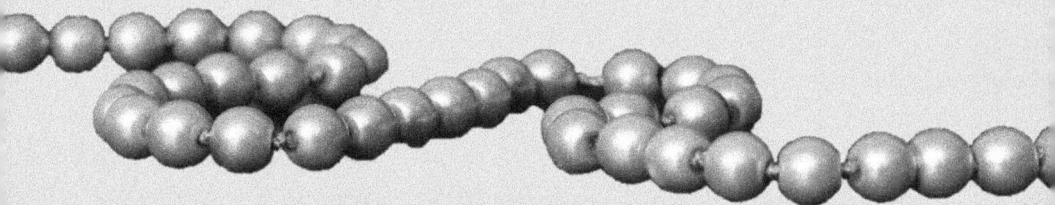

"We must develop and maintain the capacity to forgive. He who is devoid of the power to forgive is devoid of the power to love. There is some good in the worst of us and some evil in the best of us. When we discover this, we are less prone to hate our enemies."

Dr. Martin Luther King, Jr.

Pearl #2
Control Your Thoughts

Your greatest asset is your mind, for it is your strongest muscle. Just like all the other muscles in your body, you must exercise it properly in order to gain the best results. To keep your mind healthy and strong, you must ensure positive thoughts are filtered into it. Because what goes in is what will come out. On the other hand, if you fail to guard your mind from negativity, you will find yourself on a destructive path. Therefore, you need to control your thoughts by not allowing them to become captive to or controlled by the enemy. When the enemy wages war against humanity, the first thing he goes after is the mind. If he can control your mind, obtaining control over everything else is downhill from there.

"If Satan can get you to believe a lie, then he can begin to work in your life to lead you into sin. This is why he attacks the mind, and this is why we must protect our minds from the attacks of the wicked one. *'Finally, brethren, whatever is true, whatever is honorable, whatever is right, whatever is pure, whatever is lovely, whatever is of good repute, if there is any excellence and if anything worthy of praise, dwell on these things'* (Philippians 4:8)" (Wiersbe, 1979, p. 6).

In this verse, Apostle Paul admonishes us to keep our mind trained on positive thoughts. Instead though, we allow negativity from the news, in our workplace, in our homes, in our friendships, in our families, in our country, and in the world to fill our eye gates and our ear gates on a daily basis.

Then, we ponder what we have heard, allowing the negativity to delve further into our psyche, altering the way we think and stealing time away from what should take precedence in our lives: God and His Word. This trend leads us onto the wrong path and sometimes into acts of sin.

Take a moment and recall how sin entered into the world system. Romans 5:12 (ESV) informs us, *"Therefore, just as sin entered the world through one man, and death through sin, and in this way death came to all people, because all sinned."* Sin did not exist in the earth realm before man was created. It took a sinful act of man for sin to enter into the earth realm. But, what caused man to sin? What action took place that led to man's reaction?

"When Satan wanted to lead the first man and woman into sin, he started by attacking the woman's mind. This is made clear in 2 Corinthians 11:3 [NASB 1977]. *'But I am afraid that, as the serpent deceived Eve by his craftiness, your minds will be led astray from the simplicity and purity of devotion to Christ.'* Why would Satan want to attack your mind? Because your mind is the part of the image of God where God communicates with you and reveals his will to you. It is unfortunate that some Christians have minimized the significance of the mind, because the Bible emphasizes its importance" (Wiersbe, 1979, p. 4).

When we ignore the most vital part of us (our mind) that connects us to the Father through communication, we give the enemy an advantage over us. Apostle Paul tells us in II Corinthians 2:10-11 (ESV), *"Anyone whom you forgive, I also forgive. Indeed, what I have forgiven, if I have forgiven anything, has been for your sake in the presence of Christ, so that we would not be outwitted by Satan; for we are not ignorant of his designs."* Satan is crafty. That is for certain. However, we are not ignorant of his devices, his tricks, or his schemes. The arsenal Satan used in previous generations is still being used in this generation. Not only do we have that piece of information to our advantage, but the omniscient God is our protector. He knows what Satan will do before he does it, and He will provide ammunition for us, a place of refuge, and/or a way of escape. We only succumb to the enemy's attacks when we do not protect ourselves or when we falsely believe we are too clever to fall prey to the oldest trickster that exists.

"Only the inspired Word of God can reveal and defeat the devil's lies. We cannot reason with Satan, nor (as Eve discovered) can we even safely converse with him. Man's wisdom is no match for Satan's cunning. Our only defense is the inspired Word of God. It was this weapon that our Lord used when He was tempted by Satan in the wilderness" (Wiersbe, 1979, 27).

"Then Jesus was led up by the Spirit into the wilderness to be tempted by the devil. And after He had fasted forty days and forty nights, He then became hungry. And the tempter came and said to Him, 'If You are the Son of God, command that these stones become bread.' But He answered and said, 'It is written, "Man shall not live on bread alone, but on every word that proceeds out of the mouth of God"'. Then the devil took Him into the holy city and had Him stand on the pinnacle of the temple, and said to Him, 'If You are the Son of God, throw Yourself down; for it is written, "He will command His angels concerning You"; and "On their hands they will bear You up, so that You will not strike Your

foot against a stone."' Jesus said to him, 'On the other hand, it is written, "You shall not put the Lord your God to the test."' Again, the devil took Him to a very high mountain and showed Him all the kingdoms of the world and their glory; and he said to Him, 'All these things I will give You, if You fall down and worship me.' Then Jesus said to him, 'Go, Satan! For it is written, "You shall worship the Lord your God, and serve Him only."' Then the devil left Him; and behold, angels came and began to minister to Him" (Matthew 4:1-11).*

"Our Lord did not use His divine power to defeat Satan. He used the same weapon that is available to us today: the Word of God. Jesus was led by the Spirit of God and filled with the Word of God. The Word of God is 'the sword of the Spirit' (Ephesians 6:17); and the Holy Spirit can enable us to wield that sword effectively. If we are going to defeat Satan's lies, we must depend on the Word of God. This fact lays several responsibilities upon us" (Wiersbe, 1979, 29).

WE MUST <u>KNOW</u> GOD'S WORD. "There is no reason why any believer should be ignorant of the Bible. The Word of God is available to us in many translations. We have the Holy Spirit within us to teach us the truths of the Word (John 16:13-15). There are a multitude of Bible study helps available. We can turn on the radio and listen to excellent preachers and Bible teachers expound God's Word. In local churches, there are pastors and teachers who minister the Word; and in many areas, there are seminars and Bible study groups for further study. If [we, as believers,] today do not know the Bible, it is our own fault!" (Wiersbe, 1979, 29).

This means, of course, we must take time to read and study the Bible. No one will master God's Word in a lifetime of study, but we should learn all we can. We must make time, not "find time," to read and study the Word of God. Just as a machinist studies the shop manual, and the surgeon studies his medical texts, so the Christian must study the Word of God. Bible study is not a luxury; it is a necessity (Wiersbe, 1979, 29).

WE MUST <u>LEARN</u> GOD'S WORD. "Our Lord did not have a concordance with Him in the wilderness! He reached back into the Books of Moses, selected Deuteronomy, and quoted three verses from that book to silence Satan" (Wiersbe, 1979, 30).

"Your word I have treasured in my heart, that I may not sin against You" (Psalm 119:11).

"The law of his God is in his heart; his steps do not slip" (Psalm 37:31).

"I delight to do Your will, O my God; Your Law is within my heart" (Psalm 40:8).

WE MUST <u>MEDITATE</u> ON GOD'S WORD. Meditation is to the inner man what digestion is to the outer man. If we did not digest our food, we would fall sick and die.

"This book of the law shall not depart from your mouth, but you shall meditate on it day and night, so that you may be careful to do according to all that is written in it; for then you will make your way prosperous, and then you will have success" (Joshua 1:8).

"But his delight is in the law of the LORD, and in His law he meditates day and night" (Psalm 1:2).

Do you sincerely delight in the Word of God, or do you read it only out of duty? Do you rush through your "morning devotions," or take time to feed on God's truth? Measure yourself by these statements by the psalmist:

"How sweet are Your words to my taste! Yes, sweeter than honey to my mouth!" (Psalm 119:103).

"I rise before dawn and cry for help; I wait for Your words. My eyes anticipate the night watches, that I may meditate on Your word" (Psalm 119:147-148).

"I have rejoiced in the way of Your testimonies, as much as in all riches" (Psalm 119:14).

"The law of Your mouth is better to me than thousands of gold and silver pieces" (Psalm 119:72).

"Therefore I love Your commandments above gold, yes, above fine gold" (Psalm 119:127).

WE MUST <u>USE</u> GOD'S WORD. "The believer's mind should become like a 'spiritual computer.' It should be so saturated with Scripture that when he/she faces a decision or a temptation, he/she automatically remembers the Scriptures that relate to that particular situation. It is the ministry of the Holy Spirit to bring God's Word to our minds when we need it" (Weirsbe, 1979, 31).

"But the Helper, the Holy Spirit, whom the Father will send in My name, He will teach you all things, and bring to your remembrance all that I said to you" (John 14:26).

We may not be able to outthink the master manipulator, but we can take our instructions on how to combat his trickery and schemes by reading God's Word and preparing ourselves for the spiritual battle that lies ahead. Apostle Paul cautions us in II Corinthians 10:3-5 (KJV), which says, *"For though we walk in the flesh, we do not war after the flesh: (For the weapons of our warfare are not carnal, but mighty through God to the pulling down of strong holds;) Casting down imaginations, and every high thing that exalteth itself against the knowledge of God, and bringing into captivity every thought to the obedience of Christ."*

Thoughts come, and thoughts go. When negative, hurtful, debilitating thoughts arise, we have the power, authority, and ability to eradicate the thought from our mind. "We need to learn for ourselves and teach others how to guard, strengthen, and renew their minds because the battle [against] sin always starts in the mind" (Warren, 2022).

How do we rid ourselves of worldly thinking that is so often overwrought with negativity? The answer is in Romans 12:2, which says, *"And be not conformed to this world: but be ye transformed by the renewing of your mind, that ye may prove what is that good, and acceptable, and perfect, will of God."*

We cannot afford to think the way the world thinks (carnally). So, in order to have the mind of Christ, we must transform our thinking. Then, we will be able to prove what is the good, acceptable, perfect will of God.

According to Pastor Rick Warren (2022), we can transform our mind by doing two things:

1. **First, listen to God's Word more than the world.** Psalm
   1:1-3 says, *"Happy are those who . . . find joy in obeying the
   Law of the LORD, and they study it day and night. They are
   like trees that grow beside a stream, that bear fruit at the
   right time, and whose leaves do not dry up. They succeed in
   everything they do"* (GNT). Would you like those
   characteristics to be true of your life? If so, then meditate
   on God's Word every day. And, watch your life begin to
   change over time.

2. **Second, think about what you think about.** Instead of
   automatically accepting every thought you have, challenge
   your thoughts. When you have a thought, ask questions
   such as: Do I *want* to think about this? Is this really true? Is
   this helpful? How does it make me feel - and do I want to
   feel that way? II Corinthians 10:5 tells us to *"take every
   thought captive and make it obey Christ"* (GNT). All your
   feelings are caused by thoughts. If you don't like the way
   you feel, then you need to change the way you think. Simply
   take the thought causing bad feelings and replace it with a
   different thought. Proverbs 4:23 says, *"Be careful how you
   think; your life is shaped by your thoughts"* (GNT).

Why is it so important that we learn how to manage our
mind? According to Pastor Rick Warren (2022), there are three
reasons.

1. **Manage your mind because your thoughts control your life.** Proverbs 4:23 says, *"Be careful how you think; your life is shaped by your thoughts"* (GNT). Your thoughts have tremendous ability to shape your life for good or for bad. For example, maybe you accepted the thought someone told you when you were growing up: "You're worthless. You don't matter." If you accepted that thought, even though it was wrong, it shaped your life.

2. **Manage your mind because the mind is the battleground for sin.** All temptation happens in the mind. Paul says in Romans 7:22-23, *"I love to do God's will so far as my new nature is concerned; but there is something else deep within me, in my lower nature, that is at war with my mind and wins the fight and makes me a slave to the sin that is still within me. In my mind I want to be God's willing servant, but instead I find myself still enslaved to sin"* (TLB).

3. **Manage your mind because it is the key to peace and happiness.** An unmanaged mind leads to tension; a managed mind leads to tranquility. An unmanaged mind leads to conflict; a managed mind leads to confidence. An unmanaged mind leads to stress. (When you don't try to control your mind and the way you direct your thoughts, you will have an enormous amount of stress in your life.) But a managed mind leads to strength, security, and serenity.

Instead of re-playing old conversations over and over again in your mind, confront those thoughts. What you think about is *your* choice, and you don't have to believe every thought you have. When you confront a thought that you know isn't true, you can choose to change what you are thinking! You can replace it with God's truth. The only way to know truth is to get into God's Word. The more time you choose to spend in God's Word, the more His truth will help you change your thoughts. A positive change in your thoughts will lead to a healthy change in your emotional state and a positive change in your actions.

According to Covenant Keepers, we must understand the connection between our feelings, our thought life, and our behavior. Our feelings are directly associated with our thoughts. If we want to control our feelings, we must first control our thought life. Mark 14:72 declares Peter wept when he thought about his denial of Jesus. Notice how his feelings and emotions were directly controlled by what he thought.

In Lamentations 3:19-20, when Jeremiah remembered all of his afflictions, he said, "My soul...sinks within me." When Jeremiah speaks of his soul sinking, he is undoubtedly referring to his emotional state. However, when he thought on God's mercies, he experienced hope within his mind (Lam. 3:21-23).

David explains this same connection between his thoughts and feelings in Psalm 73:16. When he incorrectly thought that the wicked would escape the judgment of God, it was too painful for him. He became upset and angry. However, when he went into the sanctuary of God and turned his thoughts toward heaven (vs. 17-28), the Lord gave him a new perspective and he found strength (vs. 26).

Our feelings are directly associated with our behavior. If we want to control our feelings, we must also change our behavior. When our behavior is sinful, our conscience will accuse us. These accusations enter our mind through our thoughts and then affect our feelings and emotions.

In Romans 2:15, Paul teaches that our conscience uses our thoughts to either accuse us or excuse us. Sinful behavior without repentance will naturally cause accusing thoughts, which result in depressed feelings. Godly behavior demonstrated by obedience to God's Word will result in just the opposite feelings. Godliness results in thoughts that excuse us, which make us feel good about our actions.

In Philippians 4:8-9, Paul instructs, "The things which you learned and received and heard and saw in me, these do, and the God of peace will be with you." Note Paul believed if we would follow his example and do what he did, we would experience the peace of God.

Similarly, Jesus gave the same exhortation for how to be happy. After teaching the disciples to be servants, He said, "If you know these things, happy are you if you do them" (John 13:17). Jesus taught that happiness would naturally result from doing what we know is right. Therefore, we shouldn't wait until we feel like doing what is right. Take the biblical action commanded, and our feelings will follow.

Today is a great day to start changing your thinking. It will give you a fresh start, and eventually, it will change your life into one that is more fulfilling, productive, loving, kind, compassionate, passionate, and joyful.

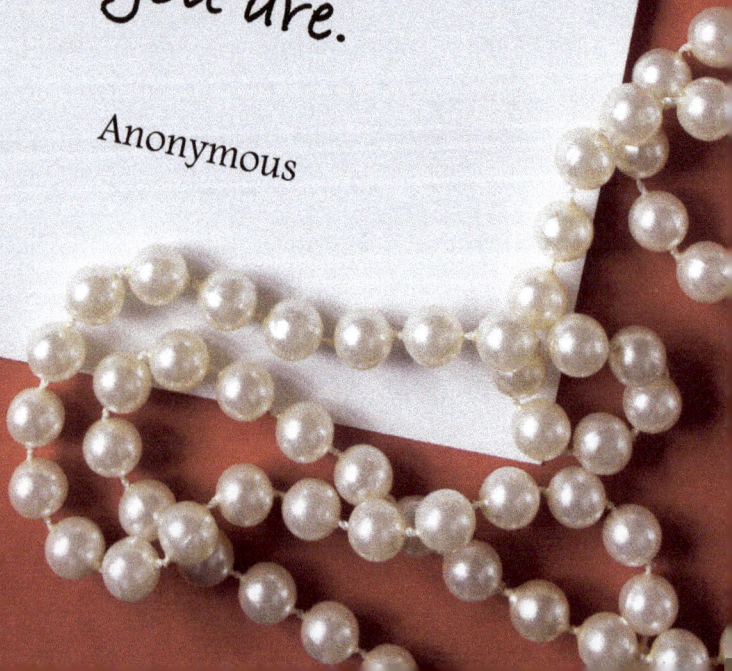

Stop focusing on how STRESSED you are, and remember how BLESSED you are.

Anonymous

It takes empathy, patience, and compassion to overcome anger, hatred, and resentment.

Dr. Martin Luther King, Jr.

The Serenity Prayer

God grant me the serenity
To accept the things I cannot change;
Courage to change the things I can;
And wisdom to know the difference.

Living one day at a time;
Enjoying one moment at a time;
Accepting hardships as the pathway to peace;
Taking, as He did, this sinful world
As it is, not as I would have it;
Trusting that He will make all things right
If I surrender to His Will;
So that I may be reasonably happy in this life
And supremely happy with Him
Forever and ever in the next.
Amen.

(Prayer attributed to Reinhold Neibuhr)

Pearl #3
Finding Inner Peace & Serenity

Inner peace is defined as the state of physical and spiritual calm despite many stressors. Serenity is the state of being calm, peaceful, and untroubled despite circumstances that may present contrary mental, emotional, and physical feelings and experiences. Finding peace of mind and serenity means finding joy, contentment, and bliss no matter how hard life can become. Finding serenity and inner peace does not depend on a problem-free life or the absence of conflict because we all experience problems in our lives.

Finding peace of mind results in fewer worries, anxieties, stress, and fears. Inner peace is linked to achieving self-actualization, which is the realization or fulfillment of one's talents and potential. God has given us all talents and abilities. Knowing what they are and functioning in them provides inner peace and a serene countenance. This, of course, is not the only way to inner peace. There are many paths that will lead to the same outcome.

Finding inner peace and serenity can have the following results.

- Better everyday function in handling your day-to-day affairs.
- Boost energy levels and better management of your emotions.
- Less drama, fewer worries, less stress, and positive thoughts.
- A kind and compassionate treatment toward other people.

- You're not affected by the negative comments of society.
- You'll learn how to deal with difficult emotions.
- The ability to have clear judgment when dealing with stressful challenges.
- Getting a good night's sleep.

According to Jared Akers (2022), there are seven steps to inner peace.

Step 1: Awareness

The first step to inner peace and serenity is awareness about something within you that needs to change, i.e. your mindset (perceptions) about yourselves, others, or the world at large or your behaviors/attitude. Romans 12:3 (KJV) says, *"For I say, through the grace given unto me, to every man that is among you, not to think of himself more highly than he ought to think; but to think soberly, according as God hath dealt to every man the measure of faith."*

Step 2: Acceptance

After becoming aware, you can move onto acceptance. You must be able to accept what it is you need to change. If you cannot get to a place of acceptance (recognizing and owning what is standing in our way), you are in denial. It's important to note that just because you accept something does not mean you have to like it. Acceptance involves responsibility.

Step 3: Identification

Once you accept what needs to change, you can identify the

areas you need to work on. Remember, just because you accept something, does not mean you have to like it, and it does not mean the process of change will be easy.

Step 4: Self-searching

This step is going to propel you into action. Are you ready? To take a good look at yourself, take out a pen and paper and start writing down things you resent and fears you have. Be honest with yourself. I Corinthians 11:28 says, *"But let a man examine himself, and so let him eat of that bread, and drink of that cup."* Here, Apostle Paul is instructing us to examine ourselves before we partake of the Lord's Supper. However, we should consistently examine ourselves on a regular basis. Once you get all these things down on paper, look back over them one by one.

Next, think of a situation(s) in which you were involved that was disturbing or hurtful to you. What role did you play? Why did you get hurt? What did you do? After all, were you not partly to blame in the incident(s)? Take a long hard look at what your part was. In some cases, you may have had no part at all, but this is your inventory, so do not point the finger at others. If you had no part, move on while accepting that your part was simply your presence.

The amazing thing about this process is you will begin to see patterns and themes in your life. You can look back and see if you continually place yourself in situations to be hurt. Do you put unreasonable expectations on yourself and others and as a result are constantly disappointed?

The goal of this entire process is to rid ourselves of those things standing in our way towards spiritual growth. Some call it baggage or character defects. Call it whatever you want, but the reality is, they are getting in your way of real growth and causing you misery. You must rid yourself of the obstructions that are getting in the way of your usefulness to God, your fellow human beings, and yourself.

Step 5: Confession

Admitting your faults to another human being is an important step in being honest with yourself. Sometimes, not sharing your faults actually makes you sick inside. You need to release your inner most secrets and allow yourself to become free from excess weight. Hebrews 12:1 says, *"Wherefore seeing we also are compassed about with so great a cloud of witnesses, let us lay aside every weight, and the sin which doth so easily beset us, and let us run with patience the race that is set before us."*

This is another reason why you should share your inventory with another person. The person can help you see events in your past for what they really are - *events in your past.* Maybe you have been too hard on yourself for something you have done. Conversely, maybe something happened in your past that is influencing your behavior more than you realize. James 5:16 (KJV) says, *"Confess your faults one to another, and pray one for another, that ye may be healed. The effectual fervent prayer of a righteous man availeth much."*

Step 6: Action

You must now take action to correct any of these wrongs that you can, by listening carefully to the Holy Spirit, who will guide you in knowing which of these amends you should make. Go over your list to see if there are some things you can make right. You can offer apologies to those you may have stepped on or hurt. Remember, this moment is not about those who have hurt you. It is about your actions and about any damage you may have caused to others.

Sometimes, the damage you caused may have been a direct or indirect result of being hurt. Hurting people hurt others. So, what you want to do is correct offenses you have caused. Romans 12:17-19 warns us, *"Do not repay anyone evil for evil. Be careful to do what is right in the eyes of everyone. If it is possible, as far as it depends on you, live at peace with everyone. Do not take revenge, my dear friends, but leave room for God's wrath, for it is written: 'It is mine to avenge; I will repay,' says the Lord."*

Step 7: Maintenance

After having gone through the first six steps, something has happened. You have felt your existence come into peace with the world around you. You can look the world in the eye and know you have done the best you could. You have laid the foundation with which real spiritual growth and joy will spring. You will find that you no longer need to say or do things which are harmful to others. Actions and words - used only to hurt others and inflate yourself - are no longer needed. For everything you need is within yourself as an individual. Maintenance is about living each day to the best of your ability. Each day, set out to bring joy and love to the lives of others. Make this your daily motto, "Today, I will only give and receive love."

In addition to navigating through the seven steps, attend to the following six areas to continue smoothing out any rough corners that tend to delay or disturb your peace of mind.

Meditation

Meditation has many proven benefits for our physical, emotional, and mental health. In particular, practicing mindful meditation decreases anxiety and prevents depression. As a believer, meditating on God's Word is always helpful and calming. Through His Word, we become in tune with His promises, His lovingkindness, His grace, and His mercy. From our knowledge and understanding of His care for us, we can find peace. Isaiah 23:6 (KJV) says, *"Thou wilt keep him in perfect peace, whose mind is stayed on thee: because he trusteth in thee."*

Be Grateful

Finding your peace and taking care of your well-being means being grateful for what you have, not what you lack in life. When you appreciate what you have in life, you'll find more peace. It has been found that individuals with a grateful heart and the those who are content with their life's blessings find peace and happiness within. James 1:17 (NIV) says, *"Every good and perfect gift is from above, coming down from the Father of the heavenly lights, who does not change like shifting shadows."*

Take Responsibility for Your Actions

Taking responsibility and accountability for all your actions takes a certain level of maturity. Even when it's hard, you'll find peace and happiness by admitting your mistakes. Accept criticisms and use them to improve yourself; accepting that you have made mistakes and unwise choices makes you a more resilient person.

Don't Let Your Past Mistakes Define You

We all have made mistakes in the past of which we are not proud. Romans 3:22b-24 reminds us, *"There is no difference between Jew and Gentile, for all have sinned and fall short of the glory of God, and all are justified freely by his grace through the redemption that came by Christ Jesus."*

But, if you dwell on your past mistakes, they will get the best of you. Don't let your past mistakes define you, and don't let those memories stop you from growing into a better individual. To find your peace and serenity, let your regrets go; do not hold on to them. Remember, those mistakes made you a better person. Moreover, you're going to commit mistakes in the future. When they occur, pick yourself up and move on.

Love Yourself

Self-care is important to finding peace and serenity. How can you be truly happy in life if you're unable to love yourself? Loving yourself means looking after your physical, emotional, mental, and spiritual health. These include eating healthy, exercising regularly, and looking after your overall well-being. When you have a healthy relationship with yourself and practice self-care, you can project this positive energy towards others as well. Mark 12:31a tells us about the second greatest commandment: *"The second is this: 'Love your neighbor as yourself.'"*

Just imagine how happy and peaceful your life can be when you feel good about yourself, and you have a healthy relationship with the people around you.

Practice Acceptance and Contentment

In the pursuit of finding peace and serenity, acceptance and contentment are key. Accept that you will have problems in your life and learn how to deal with them.

Always remember, you are a child of the King, and He cares for you. Recite Psalm 23 and allow your spirit to be at peace.

Psalm 23

The LORD is my shepherd; I shall not want.
He maketh me to lie down in green pastures: he leadeth me beside the still waters.
He restoreth my soul: he leadeth me in the paths of righteousness for his name's sake.
Yea, though I walk through the valley of the shadow of death, I will fear no evil: for thou art with me; thy rod and thy staff they comfort me.
Thou preparest a table before me in the presence of mine enemies: thou anointest my head with oil; my cup runneth over.
Surely goodness and mercy shall follow me all the days of my life: and I will dwell in the house of the LORD for ever.

A smart

person knows

what to say.

A wise person

knows whether

to say it

or not.

Attract what
you expect.
Reflect what
you desire.
Become what
you respect.
Mirror what
you admire.

Everyone loves

the beautiful

fairytale time of

relationships, but

you'll never know

you really love

someone until you've

been tested by that

"one" difficult

circumstance. And,

it _always_

shows up.

Pensacola Helene

Spiritual maturity isn't measured by how high you jump in praise but how straight you walk in obedience.

Pearl #4
Eliminate the Drama

We all experience some drama in our life at one time or another whether it occurs in our home, on the job, at church, or in the parking lot of a supermarket. However, if you find yourself dealing with drama on a frequent basis, it is time to get to the bottom of it, ascertaining the root cause. Similar to all the prior chapters, you will need to look at the part you play in the dramatic episodes in which you have been involved. Quite frankly, some people thrive off drama. It excites them and keeps them going.

The reality though is drama is distracting and a waste of time. It will take your focus off important matters and will rob you of time you could be otherwise using constructively. Time is a valuable commodity of which we all have been afforded an equal amount by God Himself. And it is not His desire for us to squander it by dealing with foolishness and matters that are inconsequential.

Psalm 90:12 (KJV) says, "*So teach us to number our days, that we may apply our hearts unto wisdom.*" Numbering our days means to keep track of our time and to put it to good use. Ephesians 5:15-16 (KJV) say, "*See then that ye walk circumspectly, not as fools, but as wise, redeeming the time, because the days are evil.*" Use your time wisely because once it is gone, you cannot retrieve it nor can it be duplicated.

The following seven nuggets can assist you in determining how, when, and why drama occurs in your life and will provide pointers on how to eliminate drama from robbing your time.

1. Recognize when <u>you</u> might be creating drama (Deschene, 2021).

> *You get what you put out. If you act in a way that is*
> *positive with minimal drama, you attract the same*
> *kind of positive situations and people.*
> *~April Myers*

> *Drama usually comes from my reaction to other people's actions.*
> *I stop to think: Does this really matter in the long run,*
> *or am I just trying to be right?*
> *~Anita Grimm-Hohl*

> *I minimize drama within myself. When I'm focused*
> *and calm, so is the world around me.*
> *~Cynthia Ruprecht Hunt*

If there is drama in multiple areas of your life, be honest with yourself – *you are* the constant factor. If you are the constant factor in the different episodes that occur with different people, ask yourself this question: Am I creating the drama? If so, why? We don't do anything repeatedly unless there's something in it for us. So, what's the payoff for having drama in your life? Are you looking for attention or excitement? Did you grow up with drama and you just feel best when there's some around you because that is what you are accustomed to occurring in your life?

If you answered 'yes' to any of the questions, now aim to find alternative solutions to situations that occur so you do not have a dramatic ending. If you're looking for attention, can you get it more directly and in a healthier manner? If you're bored, what new adventure can you create in your life? Try finding a hobby in which to expend your energy.

2. Change your perspective.

Be happy about little things; let the big stuff go because I can't change any of it.
~Grace Foo

I zoom out in my mind to a point far enough away and above so that I can see things in my life for what they are. By doing this, I can see from a distance how small and unimportant the situation is in the big scope of the universe.
~Larry Stilts

Is this situation going to matter a year from now? If not, it's not worth worrying about.
~Angela Orr

A lot of the drama takes place in our own heads, and it's usually because we are too deeply immersed in a difficult situation to recognize it isn't as dire as it seems. The issue may seem important at the moment in which it is occurring, but stop and ask yourself if it is going to matter later. If not, is it worth the energy you are depositing into it?

If you feel yourself getting overwhelmed by a situation, step back and realize the feeling isn't permanent. Nothing is. The feeling of being overwhelmed will eventually pass. Instead of focusing on your feeling, try focusing on action steps, on the things you can control. What can you do today to proactively create a solution to the dilemma you are facing? It is always better to focus on healthy solutions rather than negative emotions. Emotions will not help you to achieve your goals, but emotions can lead you into making choices that could be costly later. I Peter 5:7 (KJV) encourages us to, *"Casting all your care upon him; for he careth for you."*

3. Don't feed into other people's drama.

Build a reputation for not participating in drama.
~Addy Rodriguez

Just be. Anything you resist persists. Don't add any negative or positive focus on it.
~Nikki Star

Speak less; listen more. You may have time to hear and see the drama and sidestep it.
~Alexis Benjamin

Be an observer. Not everything needs a reaction.
~Angelina PhouGui Chan-Ong

If someone repeatedly comes to you with catastrophes, give yourself a window of time when it is best for you to listen. Do not feel obligated to listen at the moment the person calls. You may need to take a moment to become mentally prepared to hear all the person is about to pour out. If you have a personal matter to attend to, allow it to be your priority before surrendering your time to someone who always has a situation that requires attention.

Also, resist the urge to jump into a pity party. It is not your responsibility to solve other people's problems. Oftentimes, people calm themselves down when other people don't validate their complaints. And, you need to ask yourself whether or not the person will actually heed your advice or not. Does he/she really want your counsel or are you just a sounding board for him/her to hear his/her own ideas? Lastly, focus on your breathing. Do not allow the person's excitement cause you to become excited as well. Your calming energy may even help him/her let go of the anxiety he/she is experiencing.

4. Reconsider unhealthy relationships.

Minimize dramatic people in your life.
~Jeff Palmer

Befriend only people with good energy
that don't promote or create drama.
~Carmen Portela

I realize that spending time by myself
is always preferable to spending time
with someone who wants drama.
Nothing wrong with a dull day.
~Stephanie Goddard

Remove the source of drama from my life.
It really is that simple.
~Claudia Jacobs

Take inventory of which people in your life leave you feeling stressed and unhappy more often than not. After making your list, there are several options you can choose from to eliminate or at least reduce the amount of drama you experience. First, you can completely disengage from a toxic relationship. Second, if you don't want to completely remove yourself from a toxic relationship, you can minimize the time you spend with the person. Third, if you don't want to change how often you see them, at least recognize what triggers drama within each relationship. Then, when the conversation moves towards a trigger, steer it to a more meaningful or pleasurable topic.

5. Be clear, open, and straightforward with other people.

Be as open and honest and communicative
as possible. Listen without reacting.
~Faith McGregor

If I have an issue with someone, I go straight
to them to talk about it, and I don't talk to
anyone else about it if they aren't involved.
Gossip breeds drama!
~Kristie Sherman

Drama comes about because of either misunderstanding
or overreaction. Be as honest and open in all cases as
possible. Quell your own negative emotions, which will
in turn diffuse the negative emotions of others.
~Vito Ruiz

A lot of drama comes from poor communication and confusion. Eliminate it by finding the courage to say exactly what you mean. It may be harder in the moment, but it can save a lot of heartache in the long run. Conversely, let people know they can be honest with you. If people think they need to walk on eggshells around you, they will likely hold things in or sugar coat them. Overtime though, whatever is being held back *will* come out eventually, if not in words, in resentful actions. All of this can be avoided by having open, honest, and clear communication with those with whom we come in contact. Proverbs 13:16 (KJV) admonish, *"Every prudent man dealeth with knowledge: but a fool layeth open his folly."*

6. Be slow to label something as "drama," as it may really be important.

When it comes to people you know you love,
always take an extra moment to reconsider,
if the "problem" is actually a problem, if it's
worth making a big deal out of it.
~Christian Andersen Hauge

I realize that life is a roller-coaster and my problems
are much like others' at different times.
~Margaret I. Gibson

Love them a little more. It's who
they are. It might even be you.
~Ed Pulsifer

Don't speculate, good or bad. Simply
deal with what's actually in front of you.
~Michael Stodola

Because the occurrences of drama happen so frequently, in our hastiness, we may inadvertently label a situation as drama when it may actually be someone needing our assistance in a very serious situation. Instead of expelling mental energy judging the situation as good or bad up front, focus on being there and being a listening ear in the moment. Matthew 7:1-3 (KJV) says, *"Judge not, that ye be not judged. For with what judgment ye judge, ye shall be judged: and with what measure ye mete, it shall be measured to you again. And why beholdest thou the mote that is in thy brother's eye, but considerest not the beam that is in thine own eye?"*

After you have availed your ear, your advice and your time, leave all emotions with the person. Do not carry them with you. Remember, a lot of the drama we experience in life comes from our interpretations of the things we experience - particularly after the moments have passed. Is it really necessary for us to continue to ponder on things after a conversation is over when the situation does not involve us? When we do so, we carry the weight of others, and often times, it is unnecessary.

7. Learn from drama.

I attempt to allow the inevitable episode, extract any potential
meaning or lesson, and equally allow it to pass.
~Joel Olmstead

I try to see the learning experience in the drama. And I think of the sentence, "Without rain you can't enjoy the sunny days."
~Anja Feijen

Accept it, learn from it, and go on with life.
~Vincent Neerings

At times, it may seem as though drama is always happening to us, and that we are powerless to remove ourselves from the cause. Another perspective is that every time we find ourselves immersed in something that seems overwhelming, we have an opportunity to learn how to deal with challenges better. So rather than avoid the challenge, face it head on. Life will always involve mini fires that we feel desperate to put out. *"Do not be anxious about anything, but in every situation, by prayer and petition, with thanksgiving, present your requests to God"* (Philippians 4:6, NIV). Go slowly, pray, and use wisdom.

Don't be afraid
of losing people.
Be afraid of losing
yourself by trying to
please everyone
around you.

*When you come
out of the storm,
you won't be the
same person that
walked in. That's
what the storm
is all about.*

Haruki Murakami

Grace is when God gives
us good things that
we don't deserve.

Mercy is when He spares
us from bad things
we deserve.

Blessings are when
He is generous
with both.

Truly, we can never
run out of reasons
to thank Him.

Pearl #5
Looking Through Colored Lenses

From the moment a baby is born, his life is shaped by every situation that occurs within it. Each incident forms a memory whether that memory is remembered or suppressed. All of the circumstances that the child experiences, from the time of birth to the time of death, shapes who he is at one point in his life and who he will eventually become at other points.

One unfortunate truth most people fail to realize, understand or accept is our viewpoint of reality may not be the actual or complete truth. There is one absolute true reality, and it is held by our Creator. Only He knows the unadulterated truth. We humans, on the other hand, only know and therefore operate in our limited reality. Our reality is limited and only includes what is true for us. Why is that? Why is it that God can have the true reality of all things and we have a limited reality of the truth?

First, we live and operate in a realm where sin exists. Therefore, our reality is tainted by falsehoods, truths, and skewed perceptions, making it difficult to ascertain one from the other. Allow me to further explain by way of examples.

Example #1:

A young boy grows up in a positive home where there is a lot of love, kindness, and mutual respect. When the boy begins attending school, he is surrounded by teachers and other adults who treat him kindly, while showing care and concern for his wellbeing. At five years old, his sense of security is very strong and has been built on a solid foundation. Then, one day seemingly out of the blue, another little boy approaches him on the playground with an aggressive attitude and tries to take the basketball right out of his hands. The little boy tries to resist the aggressor as he wonders why his schoolmate is being so mean and rude. The little boy's reality of the world as a happy place has just been interrupted by a rude awakening of the harshness of the world. He has no real idea of the harshness that lurks around the edges of his young life, as that was only the first real encounter.

Notice how the boy believed life to be one way as a result of his prior experiences, but soon learned (in kindergarten) that life was not as he understood it to be.

Later that day, when he went home and shared with his parents the incident that transpired earlier at school, his parents realized they had not prepared their son for the cruelties that lie in wait for all of us.

The young boy had an eye-opening experience early enough in life where he did not venture too far with a false sense of reality. However, the experience he had with the aggressive schoolmate caused the colored lenses of "the world is a wonderful and kind place" to shift to another reality of "beware of people" because some of them can and will hurt you. Every experience we have compounds our thoughts about the world around us and the people in it.

Example #2:

A young girl of twelve years old has grown up in a family that does not spend much family time together, and everyone pretty much does their own thing. As a result, her social skills are pretty low, which has had a tremendous impact on her academic progress. When her teachers ask her questions, she no longer attempts to respond because of all the teasing her classmates have issued out. She has been labeled as a slow-thinking stutterer. Her self esteem is low, and she is introverted.

One day as she is walking home alone, a man comes alongside of her, walking his cocker spaniel. The man allows his pace to match the girl's. The young girl shrinks back from fear of the stranger. She has never seen him before, and she knows enough to beware of strangers. Suddenly, she stops walking and stares up at the man. He looks at her and gives her a gentle smile. Still, she remains cautious. He asks if she wants to pet the dog when he notices she is glancing in the dog's direction. She doesn't answer verbally; she only shakes her head slightly, from side to side.

The man realizes she is fearful, so he tells her to have a nice day and moves on. Standing there on the sidewalk, the girl eventually begins walking again. Shortly thereafter, she catches up with a group of girls who are talking loudly, giggling, and laughing as most tweens and teenagers do. She recognizes most of them from school. She slows her pace, not wanting to get too close. She is not in the mood for ridicule. She wants to walk home peacefully.

Just as she feared, one of the girls turns around and sees her walking timidly a few paces behind the group. The girl acts as if she does not see the other one looking at her. She pretends to be engaged in her fingernail polish. The other girl calls her by name. Shyly she looks up, realizing she cannot avoid the girl.

Just as she lifts her eyes, the other girls in the group turn around. Surprisingly, they all smile at her. That is completely unexpected. All the girls stop walking, so she can catch up with them. She stops walking too, wondering what is going to happen next. The first girl who turned around and called her name waves her up to the group. Still, she hesitates. The other girl invites her to walk with them.

Reluctantly, she joins them, expecting the worst. She just wants to be left alone. The girls start talking to her as though they had just had a wonderful experience together the day before, or as if they had just spoken to her on the phone last night. Then, one of the girls takes her cell phone out and asks for her phone number, so she can join their group text. Meanwhile, another girl touches her hair and compliments her on her hairstyle. All the girls are nice to her. She is utterly shocked. She does not know why they are being so nice to her. Her entire family and many of the other students have always treated her as an outcast.

Just as with the little boy, the girl's experiences shape her reality and her viewpoint of the world. She never expected to be loved or treated with mutual respect. After that one experience, inside of her, an empty well began to be filled with hope for days that had a bit of happiness within them.

At the beginning of this chapter, I began with the scenario of a newborn child who is essentially a blank canvas. That blank canvas begins to take shape by each experience that is written upon it, whether positive or negative. The way a person acts or thinks is predicated upon all the prior experiences.

However, should people rely upon prior experiences as a determinant of how they should respond in specific situations? It has been said, "Experience is the best teacher." But, is one's experience the absolute determiner of the outcome of a situation? Of course not. We can see from the two provided examples that what one person expected to happen (based on the prior experiences) did not transpire.

The young boy expected his schoolmate to be kind towards him. He was shocked by the boy's treatment of hostility and aggression. Those particular traits had not been demonstrated towards the boy before. So, his first experience in an adverse situation was devastating.

At the same time, the tween girl had endured a life void of affection, concern, and care beyond the basics needed for life. While her parents obviously cared for her enough to feed, clothe, and educate her, she did not experience the kind of love that provides emotional and psychological security. As a result, she had adapted to a life of solitude, even at a young age. The last thing she expected was for someone to invite her into a circle of friendship, where the participants actually like each other and demonstrate care and concern for one another.

If she was fortunate to continue to receive acceptance and kindness, her life could head onto a different track. Otherwise, her vision of reality would continue to be skewed, as she would view the world as a harsh cruel place where she has no value.

God, the Creator, did not create anyone who was void of value. Everything and everyone God created is valuable. However, your life experiences shape your reality, your mindset, your emotions, and your connectivity to the world around you.

Abuse victims have an altogether different reality. No matter how much love they are shown, they are never convinced that a person loves them unconditionally. Their unbelief can ruin a relationship simply by the thoughts they hold to be true. It does not matter what they project on the outside: strength, wisdom, responsibility, etc. On the inside, if they do not receive the proper healing, they remain broken. Eventually, the brokenness will permeate all aspects of their lives and potentially the lives of others.

Broken people often live broken and disfigured lives when they remain in a broken condition. Their thoughts toward reality are drastically skewed as a result of their experiences, causing them to view life through colored lenses. Although our experiences shape who we are and how we view the world, we can unlearn behaviors, change attitudes, and alter beliefs that are unhealthy.

To some degree, we all view life through colored lenses. It is an unfortunate reality. However, when your perception is far removed from reality, a problem exists that must be addressed.

Let's look at a few helpful steps to correct one's view of reality.

1. Get professional counseling. Talking to a professional about your viewpoints on specific topics can provide a listening ear to someone who is well grounded in reality. This person can listen and find potential flaws in your analyses or logic and show you where your reasoning may be faulty. Doing this on a consistent basis can help you with guiding your thoughts on a regular basis. *"Blessed is the man that walketh not in the counsel of the ungodly"* (Psalm 1:1, KJV).

2. Avoid making rash decisions based on how you feel. Emotions can lead to irrational thoughts, which could in turn lead to irrational and detrimental behaviors. Where do the emotions stem from? We all have triggers from our past that cause us to react. Usually prior to reacting, there was a thought. The thought then set off an emotion, and the emotion led to a response. The response was the reaction that was needed to overcome the feelings. If one is not careful, the action can lead to another thought or emotion, and one can find himself in a never-ending cycle of irrational thoughts, emotions, and behaviors. When you begin to feel unhealthy emotions rise up within you, take a moment to get hold of your emotions instead of allowing them to dictate your thoughts and vice versa. *"Casting down imaginations, and every high thing that exalteth itself against the knowledge of God, and bringing into captivity every thought to the obedience of Christ"* (II Corinthians 10:5).

3. Watch the company you keep. People who encourage your negative behaviors should be limited to the amount of time they spend with you. Negative influences rub off. Many times when we are thinking or acting contrary to how we should and someone is encouraging us, we engage in the behavior more freely. When you know behaviors, mindsets, and actions are unhealthy, refrain from spending time with those who encourage your harmful antics. *"But now I have written unto you not to keep company, if any man that is called a brother be a fornicator, or covetous, or an idolator, or a railer, or a drunkard, or an extortioner; with such an one no not to eat"* (I Corinthians 5:11, KJV).

Allow the Lord to be your guide in all you do. He will guide you by ordering your steps (Psalm 37:23). His Word will be a lamp unto your feet and a light unto your path (Psalm 199:105). And, He will pour out wisdom unto you liberally (James 1:5-6). Everything we need is in Him (II Peter 1:3).

We have the power over our own life, and we will not surrender to the adversary, who comes to steal, kill, and destroy. Jesus came to give us an abundant life (John 10:10). We can walk in abundance by changing our mindset and by refusing to fall victim to the realities of our past. We must learn how to live in the here and now, surrendering all things to the Lord. Our past will dictate our future only when we allow it to. We must take what is good and positive and discard the bad and negative. Then, we will be able to live a full healthy life as we look positively toward our future. Making the necessary changes will lead to the removal of the colored lenses, causing us to view situations accurately.

References

Akers, Jared. (2022). "How to Be Happy and Live Fearless by Overcoming Fear, Stress, and Anxiety."

Berg, Yehuda. (2011). huffpost.com.

Carr, Steve. (2022). Covenant Keepers. covenantkeepers.org

Deschene, Lori. (2021). tinybuddha.com.

Warren, Rick. (2022). PastorRick.com

Wiersbe, Warren. (1979). The Strategy of Satan. Tyndale House Publishers. Illinois.

Gift of Salvation for Non-Believers

"For all have sinned, and come short of the glory of God." (Romans 3:23)

This section was written especially for non-believers, those who have not accepted the gift of salvation. The gift of salvation saves souls from eternal damnation and is a free gift offered by God Himself.

John 3:16-18 says, *"For God so loved the world, that he gave his only begotten Son, that whosoever believeth in him should not perish, but have everlasting life. For God sent not his Son into the world to condemn the world; but that the world through him might be saved. He that believeth on him is not condemned: but he that believeth not is condemned already, because he hath not believed in the name of the only begotten Son of God."*

This section of scripture tells us God's purpose for giving His son Jesus to the world. The world was in a bad condition. The world was overwrought with sin; the people were living for fleshly desires rather than for God's desires.

As a result of the world's conditions, God decided He would offer the perfect sacrifice that would save the world from being a place where people were lost and had no hope. He decided His own son could stand in proxy for the sin-filled world, taking all sin upon Himself.

So Jesus came, born of a virgin, to save this dying world. He walked on this earth for 33 ½ years, doing the work of His Heavenly Father. At the appointed time, He died by way of crucifixion upon a cross at Calvary, on Golgotha's hill. He shed His blood and died for you and for me. Because His blood was pure, it paid the penalty for all unrighteousness and gave those who believe in Him direct access to His father's throne.

Scripture tells us in Matthew 27:51 that the veil of the temple was ripped in two from top to bottom, at the moment that Jesus' spirit left His body. As a result of the veil's removal, we are no longer required to have a high priest make intercession for us. We, as the children of the Most High God, are able to approach the throne of God for ourselves, and Jesus sits on the right hand of the Father making intercession for us.

But what is even more miraculous than God offering His own son as the perfect sacrifice was the fact that when Jesus was placed in grave clothes and placed in a tomb, He only remained there until the third day. God would not have it that His son would remain in the heart of the earth forever. In order for people to believe in the awesome power of God and His dear son Jesus, a miracle had to be performed. So, on the third day, after Jesus died on the cross, He was resurrected, demonstrating the omnipotence of God.

This very act was the act that would cause people to believe in a god that reigns supreme and holds the power of the universe in His very hands, a god that could save them from themselves.

Today, if you are an unbeliever, you can change your destiny. You can change where you will spend your eternity. Our Heavenly Father gives us the freedom of choice about how we want to live our life here on earth and how we want to spend eternity. In Deuteronomy 30:19, God boldly declares, *"I call heaven and earth to record this day against you, that I have set before you life and death, blessing and cursing: therefore choose life, that both thou and thy seed may live."*

So, dear friend what choice will you make today? Will you spend your eternity with the Creator or will you suffer Hell's eternal flames? Again, the choice is yours. Just as the men aboard the ship who were with Jonah became believers, you too can make a choice to accept the only one and true living God as your god.

If after reading the above passages, you have decided that you want to spend your eternity in Heaven with God, the creator, and His son Jesus, and the Holy Spirit, read through what has affectionately come to be known as the Roman's Road. This is the road to salvation. As you read through the scriptures that comprise the Roman's Road, you will also read the explanation for each scripture, so you will have clarity about what you are reading and confessing.

The Roman's Road to Salvation

The road to salvation begins with Romans 3:23 which declares, *"For all have sinned, and come short of the glory of God."* This scripture explains that everyone has come short of God's glory and needs redemption. Then, Romans 6:23a states, *"For the wages of sin is death."* Here, we learn that the consequence of living a life of sin is death. Everyone will experience physical death as a result of the sin committed in the garden of Eden, but those who commit themselves to a life of sin will suffer eternal damnation in the lake of fire (Rev. 19). Continue with the rest of verse 6:23 that says, *"but the gift of God is eternal life through Jesus Christ our Lord."* There is an alternative to suffering eternal damnation. We can accept the gift of salvation by accepting Jesus as our personal Lord and Savior. Then, Romans 5:8 says, *"But God commendeth his love toward us, in that, while we were yet sinners, Christ died for us."* We are able to receive the gift of salvation because Christ came to earth and shed His blood for us on the cross.

Continue to Romans 10: 9-10 which says, *"That if thou shalt confess with thy mouth the Lord Jesus, and shalt believe in thine heart that God hath raised him from the dead, thou shalt be saved. For with the heart man believeth unto righteousness; and with the mouth confession is made unto salvation."* If we confess with our mouths that Jesus is the son of God, that He came and died for our sins, and that God raised Him from the dead, we will receive salvation.

The Roman's Road to Salvation

The road to salvation begins with Romans 3:23 which declares, *"For all have sinned, and come short of the glory of God."* This scripture explains that everyone has come short of God's glory and needs redemption. Then, Romans 6:23a states, *"For the wages of sin is death."* Here, we learn that the consequence of living a life of sin is death. Everyone will experience physical death as a result of the sin committed in the garden of Eden, but those who commit themselves to a life of sin will suffer eternal damnation in the lake of fire (Rev. 19). Continue with the rest of verse 6:23 that says, *"but the gift of God is eternal life through Jesus Christ our Lord."* There is an alternative to suffering eternal damnation. We can accept the gift of salvation by accepting Jesus as our personal Lord and Savior. Then, Romans 5:8 says, *"But God commendeth his love toward us, in that, while we were yet sinners, Christ died for us."* We are able to receive the gift of salvation because Christ came to earth and shed His blood for us on the cross.

Continue to Romans 10: 9-10 which says, *"That if thou shalt confess with thy mouth the Lord Jesus, and shalt believe in thine heart that God hath raised him from the dead, thou shalt be saved. For with the heart man believeth unto righteousness; and with the mouth confession is made unto salvation."* If we confess with our mouths that Jesus is the son of God, that He came and died for our sins, and that God raised Him from the dead, we will receive salvation.

Finish with Romans 10:13, which states, *"For whosoever shall call upon the name of the Lord shall be saved."* Call upon the name of God by saying these words, **"Lord Jesus, come into my heart and save me, Lord. I believe that you are the Son of God who came and died on the cross for my sins. I believe that you rose from the grave. I also believe that you now sit in heaven on the right side of the Father, making intercession for me. I accept you as my Lord and my Savior."**

Now that you have confessed with your mouth that Jesus is the son of God and that He died for our sins and rose from the grave, **YOU ARE NOW SAVED!!!!** You will spend your eternity in heaven.

The next step is very important- you must find a Bible-based church that teaches the Word of God and confesses the Lord Jesus Christ to be the son of God. Don't delay. Do this immediately. Do not leave yourself open to the enemy. Get connected with the saints of the Most High God and keep yourself covered with the unspotted blood of the Lamb.

Here is my prayer for you.
Father God,

I thank you for the opportunity to minister your word to the unsaved, the unchurched, and the uncommitted. Father God, I pray now for the souls who have just received the gift of salvation. Lord Father, they have opened their hearts to you, and I know that you have received them into your kingdom and written their names in the Book of Life. Father God, I pray that you will touch their lives and show yourself mightily before them. Let their eyes be opened by the scales falling off, allowing them to see clearly.

Father God, I even pray for the backslider, those who have turned away from you after receiving the gift of salvation. You said in your Word that you desire that none would perish. So Lord, I send your Word to them right now, praying that they would confess the iniquity in their heart, repent, and turn from their evil ways, so that they may receive a life of abundance. You said in your Word in Matthew Chapter 14, that every knee shall bow before you and every tongue will confess that Jesus is Lord.

Father God, I pray now that we all come under subjection to your Word and that we will humbly submit our lives to you. I ask all these things in the name of my Lord and Savior Jesus Christ.
Amen, Amen, Amen!!!!

I will continue to pray for your success in your walk with God. Remember, this spiritual walk that you are about to embark on will not be an easy walk, but remember, the race is not given to the swift but to those who endure to the end.

Be blessed with heaven's best. I love you!

About the Author

Dr. Cassundra White-Elliott resides in California with her family, where as an English/Education professor, she teaches at various community colleges.

When writing, she composes with the direction of the Holy Spirit, in an effort to share with God's people all He has for them.

In addition to teaching and writing, Dr. Elliott also serves as an evangelistic teacher. She is also the founder of International Women's Commission, a ministry that serves the needs of the entire person, by attending to healing the mind, body, soul, and spirit.

Dr. Elliott holds a Ph.D. in Education, a Master's degree in English Composition, and a Bachelor's degree in Education.

Dr. Elliott is the founder and editor-in-chief for *Christian Inspiration* magazine, which covers topics germane to Christian living and the world at large.

Dr. Elliott is also the founder of CLF Publishing, LLC. For your publishing needs, go online to www.clfpublishing.org.

Other Works by the Author

(All books can be purchased at
creativemindsbookstore.com
amazon.com
barnesandnoble.com)

From Despair, through Determination, to Victory!

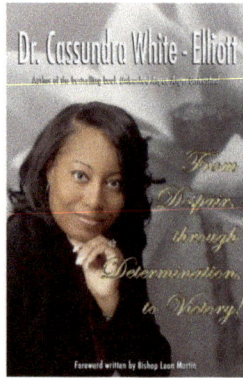

A lot can happen during a span of 40 years. The life of Dr. Cassundra White-Elliott has been anything but uneventful. From a fun-loving childhood sprinkled with incidents of abuse to a tumultuous young adulthood to a stable, secure adult life, she has experienced a full life, with much more to come. Her story is inspiring and motivating.

If anyone lacks hope, reading Dr. White-Elliott's autobiography will propel him/her into an attitude of "Maybe I can." This attitude, if nurtured and developed, will grow into an attitude of "Yes, I can." Throughout her life, Dr. White-Elliott has always held in her heart the belief that she could achieve anything that she had a made-up mind to embark upon. She was determined to achieve her heart's desires, doing what God has called her to do. She takes no credit for herself. All the glory goes to God, for He is her driving force. In Him, she lives, moves, and has her being.

Through the Storm

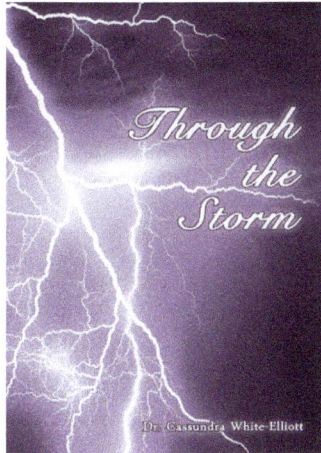

Through the Storm was duly inspired by the avaricious cloud of depression that decided to hover overhead of my daily existence in the latter part of 2007. Although I found it extremely difficult, I was once again compelled to not be defeated by just another snare that the enemy, the trickster, set for me. Once again, or more appropriately I should say *continuously*, he has exerted pernicious efforts to snatch the very life out of me by causing me to wallow in despair and to believe that I had been overcome by failure when in actuality and all reality, I was just experiencing a temporary setback. During those cloudy days, I had to remind myself daily that even though I was a target of the enemy, I am and will always be a child of the Most High God, Jehovah, who is my rock, my stability.

Unleashed Anger, Anger Unleashed

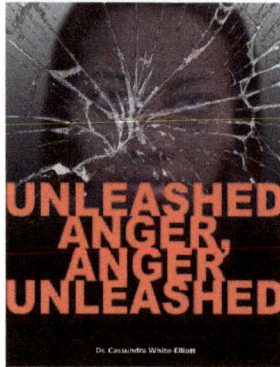

Introduction (snippet)

As I prepared to embark upon the adventure of writing this book, I had to prepare myself to also be transparent. I have found that being transparent is required in order for healing to transpire, healing for all those that peruse the pages of this book and myself. And I may as well tell you that today, at the onset of this project, I have not been totally delivered from my condition of being an anger-filled person. However, I am definitely a work in progress. I have made strides with the assistance of my Lord and Savior, Jesus Christ, who is the head of my life. Without his love, guidance, and teachings, I would not be the woman of God I am today. I shudder to think where I could be instead and will therefore not entertain the thought.

Public Speaking in the Spiritual Arena

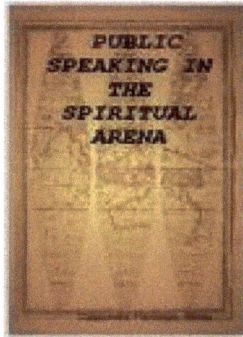

Chapter Two

How Communication Works

Purpose: This chapter will explain the six primary components of communication, identifying their purpose and how they work together.

<u>The Source</u>

In oral communication, the source of information is the speaker. In a church setting, the foundation of the message is God's word, but it is a speaker's interpretation of God's word that is delivered to the audience. As speakers vary, the information may vary but should have a similar essence because the foundational text is the same.

<u>The Message</u>

The message is the collective set of ideas that the speaker (the source) wants to deliver and/or illustrate to the audience. The message can be informative where the speaker informs the audience about a specific set of information. Or, the message may be persuasive in nature if the speaker wants to persuade the audience about conducting themselves in a specific manner, accepting God's commandments, or any number of things.

Where is Your Joppa?

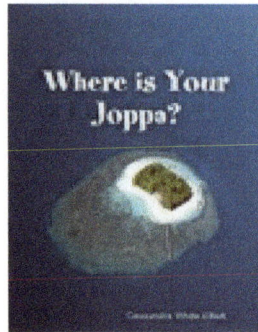

Where is Your Joppa? was written for the express purpose of illustrating God's call for obedience in the lives of believers with respect to the individual call that He has on each of our lives. As you read throughout the various chapters, notice that the emphasis is placed on our persistent disobedience in answering God's call in a specific area of our lives. We have become a people who are similar to the Israelites when they found themselves in the middle of the wilderness, following their exodus from Egypt. Before God, they murmured and complained about their current life conditions and failed to be obedient to God's statutes delivered through His servant Moses. Their persistent disobedience caused them to lose the opportunity to see and enter the Promised Land. I ask you, "What has your disobedience cost you?" "Was your disobedience worth what it cost you?" "Do you think about the souls you could have ushered into the kingdom of God?" These are some of the questions that I pray will be answered through your reading of the book.

Mayhem in the Hamptons

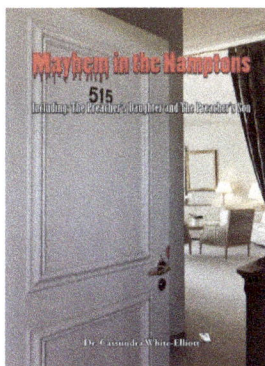

Romero and Yolanda optimistically plan for the day that is going to change their lives from being single persons to a couple who is united in holy matrimony. They, along with their parents, close friends and family, fly over to the infamous Hamptons, where only the rich and famous vacation, to have their dream wedding at the five-star Hampton Suites located on a peninsula in the Hamptons. Little do they know that their perfect day will turn out to be less than perfect when their wedding planner Mariesha Coleman suddenly goes missing!

A time when the newlyweds' lives should be filled with joy and the creation of wonderful memories, they are stricken with grief as they desperately try to find clues to help solve Mariesha's disappearance.

Mayhem in the Hamptons is a tale that shares how the horrors of a woman's past can come back to haunt her in more than one way and the impact it can have on anyone who gets in the way.

Preacher's Daughter

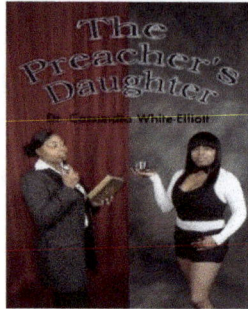

Tinisha, the daughter of a preacher, is a twenty-six-year-old God-fearing young woman endeavoring to complete law school so that she can make her mark in the courtroom. Working in one of the late-night clubs in Hollywood to earn money to pay her own way through school, Tinisha soon learns that life doesn't always go as planned. Finding her strength in her faith, Tinisha constantly finds herself praying as she watches God move miraculously in her life.

Preacher's Son

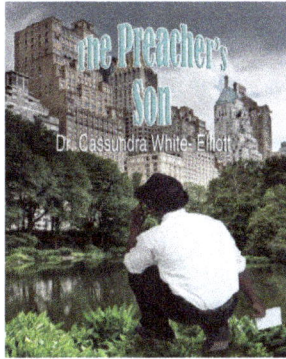

Romero Turner is a private investigator with a promising future. As he continues to build his career, he is excited about the cases he undertakes. However, his father Pastor Theodore Turner has other plans for his son's life. In the midst of trying to save his client's husband from Sylvester Domingo, a ruthless crime lord, Romero must try to salvage his relationship with his father. He must decide if ministry or life as a detective is in his future.

Lord, Teach Me to be a Blessing!

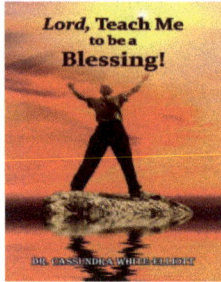

Lord, Teach Me to be a Blessing! will change a person's mentality from being centered around "me, myself, and I" to focusing on "others."

The world system teaches us that it is acceptable to place ourselves above others in an attempt to get ahead and even to survive. Herbert Spencer coined the phrase '*survival of the fittest*' after reading Charles Darwin's theory of evolution. This concept of surpassing and outdoing others is the world's philosophy.

However, the word of God does not subscribe to or promote this self-centered ideology, and therefore, neither should believers. We must hold fast to the truths outlined in Holy Scripture: "*Love thy neighbor as you love thyself*" (James 2:8) and "*It is more blessed to give than to receive*" (Acts 20:35).

While holding God's truths to be self-evident, we must demonstrate them to others, thereby showing them the way of the Lord of how to be a blessing to someone *rather* than looking to receive a blessing.

This is the very purpose of this book: to change the mentality of the world from being *self*-centered to *other* centered.

After the Dust Settles

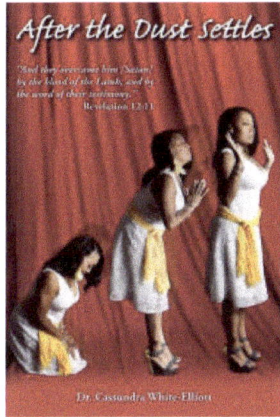

Throughout the journey of life, we all experience ups and downs and joys and pains. Most of us successfully find solutions to the situations/problems we encounter, but we often avoid dealing with the attached emotions. If we continue to ignore the emotions of pain, hurt, disappointment, anger, etc., we set ourselves up for destruction. Our families, our cultures, and our society tell us to be strong, to keep our chin up, and to grin and bear it. However, these methods of avoidance can lead us to strokes due to the undue amount of pressure we place on ourselves and/or mental illness from being unable to cope with the emotional baggage we have accumulated.

In *After the Dust Settles*, Dr. C. White-Elliott shares several situations that we all may encounter at one time or another in our lifetime and how to successfully navigate through them, so we can find ourselves emotionally healthy after the dust has settled and the situation has been rectified.

Begin reading today and experience a better tomorrow!

Claim Your Inheritance

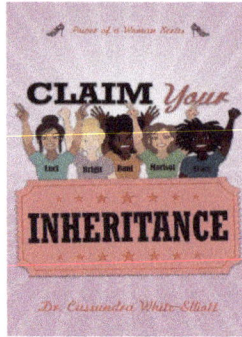

"The thief cometh not, but for to steal, and to kill, and to destroy: I am come that they might have life, and that they might have it more abundantly" (John 10:10).

Satan's mission is to steal, kill, and destroy all that God has provided for us. With him on the rampage, we must be ready to go to war- spiritually and naturally. On the other hand, we could sit idly by and allow the enemy to take what is rightfully ours. However, that is not the will of God. God has given us power to tread upon serpents and scorpions (Luke 10:19) and to reclaim all the enemy has stolen from us.

This book will share how we can be victorious in reclaiming what is rightfully ours when the enemy has turned his ugly head in our direction and made us prey for his latest scheme.

With God on our side, the enemy will not prevail!

A Diamond in the Rough

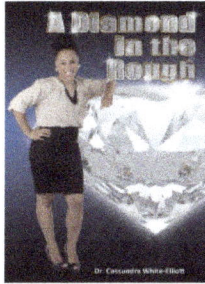

A Diamond in the Rough Architecture Firm was built and is owned and operated by lead architect Kyra Fraser. For the last five years, Kyra has been extremely successful in business, but her love life leaves much to be desired.

Kyra has set high standards for herself and does not wish to take a man in any condition and attempt to make him over. She is looking for someone who is drama free, well educated, very cultured, fun-loving, good looking, self-motivated, and the list goes on.

Will Kyra find the man of her dreams, or will her dream just continue to be a dream?

As you delve into this page-turning novel, Kyra's reality will unfold as you are drawn into her world of design, love and office drama- which includes her best friend's husband who is looking for love in all the wrong places.

365 Days of Encouragement

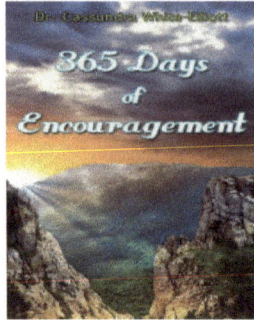

Just as our brain requires oxygen obtained from the air we breathe to sustain our mortal bodies, our spirit requires revitalization and encouragement in order to be strengthened each and every day of our lives. The revitalization and encouragement needed for the spirit of man comes directly from the word of God and assists us in walking according to the way of our heavenly Father. *365 Days of Encouragement* provides a scripture a day for each day of the year. Along with the daily scripture is a brief note of commentary also for the benefit of edifying the saints of God.

It is my prayer that the people of God would live a fulfilled life through Christ Jesus. Knowing His word and understanding we can walk in the fulfillment thereof is empowering. We are instructed in II Timothy 2:15, *"Study to shew thyself approved unto God, a workman that needeth not to be ashamed, rightly dividing the word of truth"* (KJV). Take an opportunity to delve further into the word of God, to know His statutes and to allow your own personal life to be edified, so you can be equipped to bring glory to God and lived a fulfilled life.

A Mother's Heart

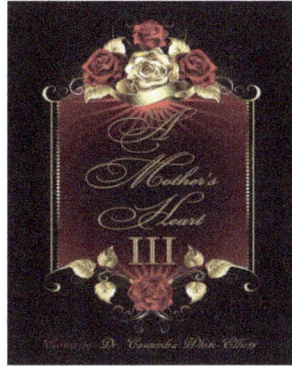

A Mother's Heart shares the unconditional love of mothers through a compilation of testimonies. Each testimony serves as a tribute to a special mother. The children of the represented mothers have lovingly written about their childhood, young adult life and/or older adult experiences they shared with their mother. As you read the writers' reflections, you will feel the expressions of love exude from the pages.

The purpose of this book is two-fold. First, it honors those mothers who stood by their children through the trials of life and showered them with unconditional love. Second, the book is a source of encouragement for mothers who may feel inadequate and question whether or not they are actually suited for motherhood. Our advice to mothers is, "Be encouraged; the journey of motherhood may seem daunting at times and you may shed some tears, but your children will never forget the love you have shown them and instilled in them to share with others."

Mothers may not be perfect, but they are definitely unmatched by any other category of person on God's green earth!

Broken Chains

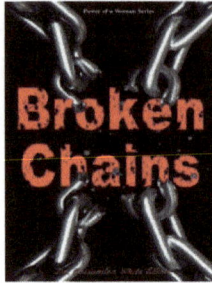

Broken Chains is an in-depth survey of five life-changing tragedies that can and will serve as chains to bind us if we are not watchful and mindful of their potential effects. In our lifetimes, we may all experience death of loved ones, sexual abuse, broken relationships, promiscuity, and sickness and disease. These everyday life occurrences can have detrimental effects on the remaining years of our lives and change our existence, unless we deal with them in a healthy manner.

Broken Chains not only brings to light the detrimental effects of five life-changing tragedies, but it also shares how anyone who experiences them can be healed and delivered from their effects.

If you have experienced death of a loved one, sexual abuse, a broken relationship, the effects of promiscuity, and/or sickness and disease and have not been able to rid yourself of the emotions attached to them or specific resulting behaviors, Broken Chains is for you.

God designed each of us for a purpose, and He has an intended end for us to achieve. In order for us to effectively achieve our God-given purpose, we must be free of chains that bind us. It is not God's desire that we become immobilized by life's events. His desire is for us to be healed, delivered and set free. Be healed today, in the name of the Lord Jesus Christ!

I Have Fallen

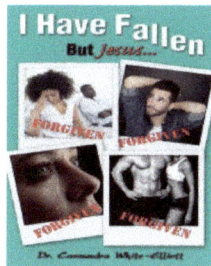

Do you know anyone who has committed his/her life to Christ but has done something unseemly that you would never expect a Christian to do? How did you feel about that person or what the person did? Did you pass judgment? What if that person were you? How would you feel if you made a misstep and no one forgave you and instead began to treat you differently? How do you feel when you are judged for past mistakes or lifestyles that are no longer part of your life?

This book shares four true stories of Christians who have made missteps during their walk with God. The purpose is not to air their dirty laundry, but to demonstrate our humanness and our vulnerability. None of us are exempt from making errors and falling into sin. It can happen to any of us.

The solution for these dilemmas is for the person who fell into sin to make a life-changing move and turn away from the sin, repent and ask God for forgiveness. His arms are waiting!

The next solution is for those who witness the sin or know of it. Pray and be of comfort to the one who has fallen. Lead him/her back to the path of righteousness. Love thy neighbor and treat him/her as you want to be treated!

The Bottom Line

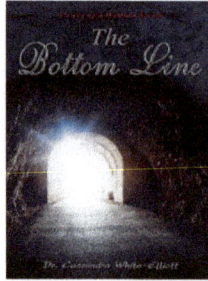

The Bottom Line is a detailed review of the Book of Job. Much can be said about Job's experiences with the loss of his children and wealth and the subsequent return of it all in mass proportions. However, the telling of Job's story in the Holy writ was not intended to focus on the return of his wealth. Instead, the focal point should be on the bottom line of the entire situation.

When you experience trials or tragedies in your life, do you tend to focus on the trial itself, the result, or the bottom line?

"What is the bottom line?" you may ask. The bottom line is the message God is sending regarding the situation.

When Job experienced his tragedies, there was a bottom line. Likewise, when you experience your trials and tragedies, there is a bottom line as well. It is up to you to discover it.

This book will reveal the bottom line in the Book of Job. It is readily apparent, but many often overlook it.

Now, it is up to you to uncover the bottom line of your experiences, for God will not bring a trial to you without a good reason.

Power of a Woman

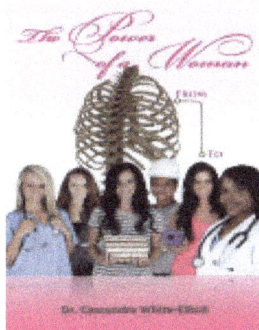

The ongoing conversation about the value of a woman is presented from a different perspective in *The Power of a Woman*. Dr. Cassundra White-Elliott presents a biblical perspective of women and compares it to the worldview of both yesterday and today. This comparison seeks to illustrate God's intended purpose for His uniquely designed creation: woman. Dr. Elliott shares God's truth about pre-imposed limitations set by man versus the limitations God Himself set for woman in addition to the wealth of liberality He gave her.

Women's creativity and abilities are not meant to be stifled. They are meant to be utilized to bring glory to God, to help sustain and nurture their families, and to move the world forward. Knowing God's truth will show women how to celebrate and appreciate who they are as well as one another!

Women, let's take the blinders off, lift our heads up, and march forward, side by side with men, and bring glory and honor to God! Take your rightful place with a gentle smile and grace and be who God called you to be!

Power of a Woman Series

Time is Running Out!

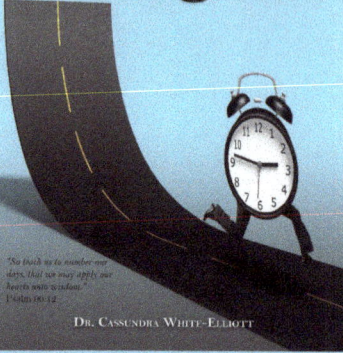

"So teach us to number our
days, that we may apply our
hearts unto wisdom."
Psalm 90:12

Dr. Cassundra White-Elliott

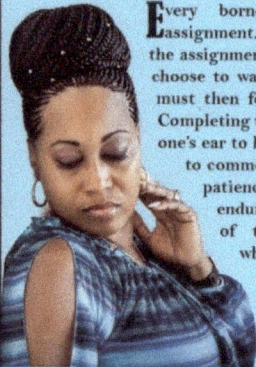

Every born-again believer has a God-given assignment. Whether or not the individual accepts the assignment is a personal decision. For those who choose to walk in God's will rather than their own must then follow God's divine plan for their life. Completing the God-given assignment means tuning one's ear to hear, receiving guidance, knowing when to commence, and, most importantly, exercising patience. Furthermore, the task may require enduring hardship along the way. A servant of the Lord can never fully anticipate what may occur during the journey of completing an assignment. What should be foremost in the individual's mind is completing the task, so he/she can hear the Master say, "Well done."

If you have never completed a God-given assignment, or if you are preparing to embark upon a new journey designed by the Lord, this book is for you. It will provide guidance for commencing and completing God-given tasks. If you feel intimidated by the task ahead, don't be dismayed. The Lord said He will never leave you or forsake you (Hebrews 13:5). Trust and believe that He will be with you every step of the way.

But you must act now!
Time is running out!

CLF Publishing, LLC.
www.clfpublishing.org

Dr. Cassundra White-Elliott's books are available at:
www.creativemindsbookstore.com
www.amazon.com
www.barnesandnoble.com

ISBN 978-1-945102-21-9
90000
9 781945 102219

Set Free

If you possess habits and display characteristics that are unbecoming, debilitating, and hinder the desired progress in your life or that affect your relationships with others, Set Free will provide the steps you need to be healed and delivered, through the Word of God.

Deliverance is available to you! Claim your healing today and walk in victory!

Do You Know God?

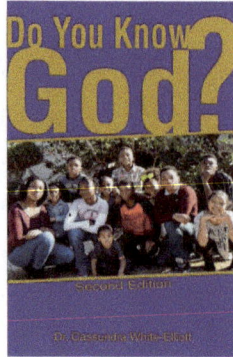

Have you or someone you know ever felt alone, confused, or unsure about your walk with God or are you unsure of what being a Christian is all about? ***Do You Know God?*** is an excellent text for providing answers to many of your questions. This book introduces adolescents and young adults to God in addition to answer many of their questions about being a Christian. This book shares the testimonies of the trials and tribulations that other teens have experienced and how God prevailed in their lives. All the information that is shared on the pages of the book is based upon the Word of God and the scriptures are taken from the King James Version of the Bible. If you are interested in knowing more about God's Word or how to begin your Christian experience, this book is for you.

Daughter, God Loves You!

"... for her price is far above rubies"
(Proverbs 31:10b)

Dr. Cassundra White-Elliott

---

*M*aybe you have heard the proclamation, "The world is going to hell in a hand basket!" Well, I believe I must concur.

However, I do *not* believe, we- the adult, mature believers- should sit idly by and allow our daughters (and our sons for that matter) to go with it! We must fight for our girls and young women, for they are the mothers of tomorrow, and some may even be young mothers today. Not only will they continue the human race, but also they can have bright futures in their careers and as leaders in our society, as they allow God to direct their paths and order their steps.

Daughter, God Loves You! is an earnest attempt to address many of the issues that plague our society and turn our daughters' heads away from God.

In this book, we dive head first into topics such as God's love, the importance and impact of education, the effects of social media, overcoming abuse, and the proper perspective of the future.

For the young adult women- Reading this book will empower you to have a bright prosperous future from being enlightened about the dangers that plague our society and how to avoid pitfalls, as you walk along the path God has paved for you.

I invite all of you to take this journey with me to save our daughters and yourselves (young women) from corruption, by being empowered with knowledge.

We must thwart the plan of the enemy. So, LET'S GO!

CLF Publishing, LLC.
www.clfpublishing.org

ISBN 978-0-9961971-9-9
90000

9 780996 197199

Web of Lies

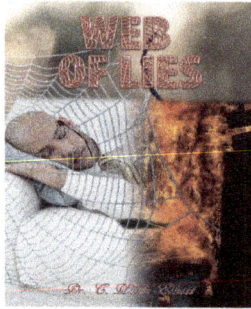

A year ago, Charlito Jimenez was found in his den, lying on the couch, with a fatal gunshot wound in his temple. Everyone in the community still wants to know who is guilty of the unfathomable crime.

Tinisha Salisbury, attorney at law, has taken the case of the accused. Can she prove her client's innocence or will a guilty verdict be rendered?

Halfway through the trial, a badly burned body was found at the scene of a fire.

Is there a string of murders being committed?

Are the murders related?

Web of Lies spins the tales of several characters into one web. Each has a story to tell, and everyone has something to hide. The web of lies, deceit, and revenge take over the lives of these characters to the point where they may not be able to see their way clear.

Embracing Womanhood

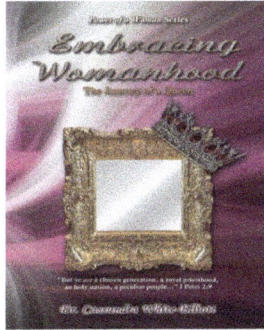

The journey from adolescence through puberty to young adulthood can be challenging and quite disconcerting for the average young lady. The changes that occur both mentally and physically can be both confusing and uncomfortable. However, the outcome of the changes can be beautiful. What she will experience during this time in her life is simply a metamorphosis – taking off the old and embracing the new. The process is similar to that of an awkward caterpillar that overtime develops into a beautiful, graceful butterfly.

The topics covered in this book (puberty, self-esteem, mental stability, goals, finances, and relationships) will assist young women (ages 15–23) in understanding the transformation they are enduring to prepare them for the life that lies ahead. After taking in the information, they will literally witness themselves evolve from princess to queen!

The Making of Dr. C.
A Memoir

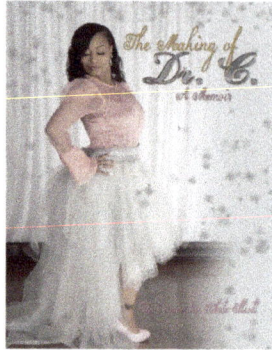

The Making of Dr. C. shares the 50-year journey of Dr. Cassundra White-Elliott. Her journey of trials, missteps, successes, and triumphs will inspire you to face any trial you may encounter with a positive attitude and the Word of God.

Her life demonstrates no matter what you may face, there is always a brighter tomorrow.

Keeping the faith will allow God to work in your life. After all, He only wants the best for you!

Prepare for Battle

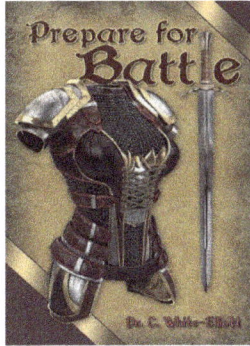

The very life you live is a war zone, riddled with battles ranging from the unexpected to the inconceivable to the paralyzing. The only way for you to successfully navigate through each battle unscathed or with minimal damage or loss is to equip yourself with the full armor of God, which consists of the girdle of truth, the breastplate of righteousness, the gospel of peace, the shield of faith, the helmet of salvation, and the sword of the spirit. To seal your victory, prayer is just as essential a component as each piece of armor. Therefore, the seven aforementioned items serve to comprise the arsenal necessary for winning wars.

This book goes to great lengths to explain each piece of armor in depth, with use of commentaries. The more you understand the importance of the arsenal, its function in battle, and how to effectively use it, the better prepared you will be when unexpected or inconceivable or paralyzing battles confront you.

Equipping yourself today for battle, with the full armor of God, will prevent Satan, our adversary, from annihilating you.

Safety in Him

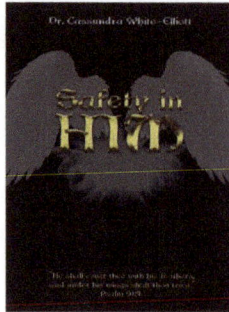

Luke 21:33 declares, *"Heaven and earth shall pass away: but my words shall not pass away,"* and Jeremiah 1:12 says, *"Then said the Lord unto me, Thou hast well seen: for I will hasten my word to perform it."* According to these two verses, we can stand firmly on the Word of God at all times because His Word is everlasting, and He watches over it continuously to perform it.

While the promises of man may go unfulfilled, God's Word is true and He declares, *"So shall my word be that goeth forth out of my mouth: it shall not return unto me void, but it shall accomplish that which I please, and it shall prosper in the thing whereto I sent it"* (Isaiah 55:11).

In this book, particular attention is brought to Psalm 91:1-7. In these verses, God promises His divine protection for His children. Read Christopher's story and see how the divine protective nature of God is demonstrated and remember Acts 10:34b, which states, *"God is no respecter of persons."* What He is able to do for one, He is able to do for another. So, no matter what you be faced with today, call on the Lord, and He will deliver you!

Women's Study Bible

NEW INTERNATIONAL VERSION

Red Letter Bible

CLF PUBLISHING, LLC

Learn the Bible Series

(26 books from A-Z to teach children biblical
principles and prominent characters.)
Currently available are A-R. More coming soon!

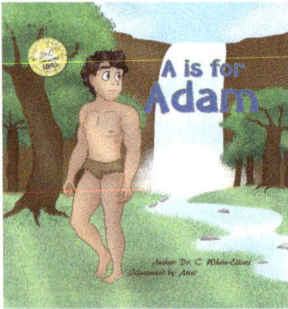

A is for Adam

B is for Babel

C is for Christ

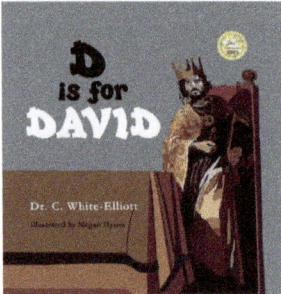

D is for DAVID

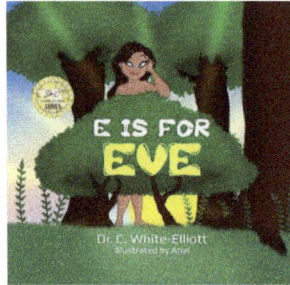

E IS FOR EVE

F IS FOR FORGIVENESS

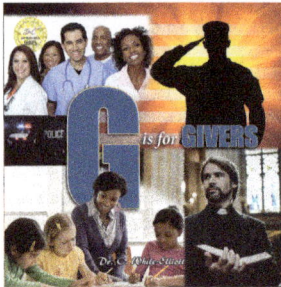

G is for GIVERS

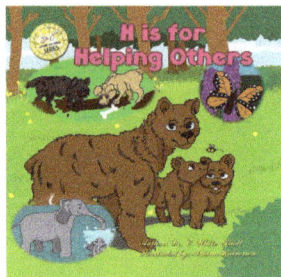

H is for Helping Others

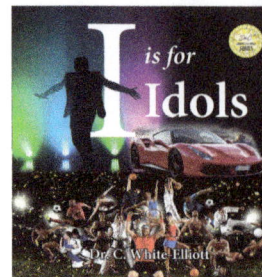

I is for Idols

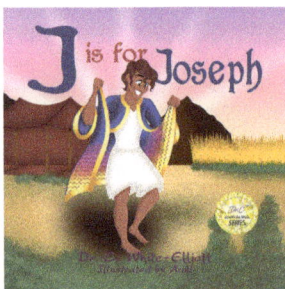

J is for Joseph

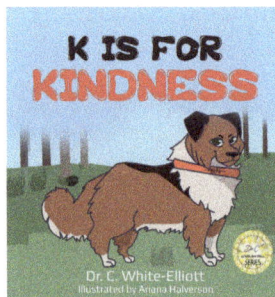

K IS FOR KINDNESS

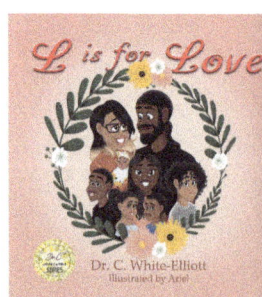

L is for Love

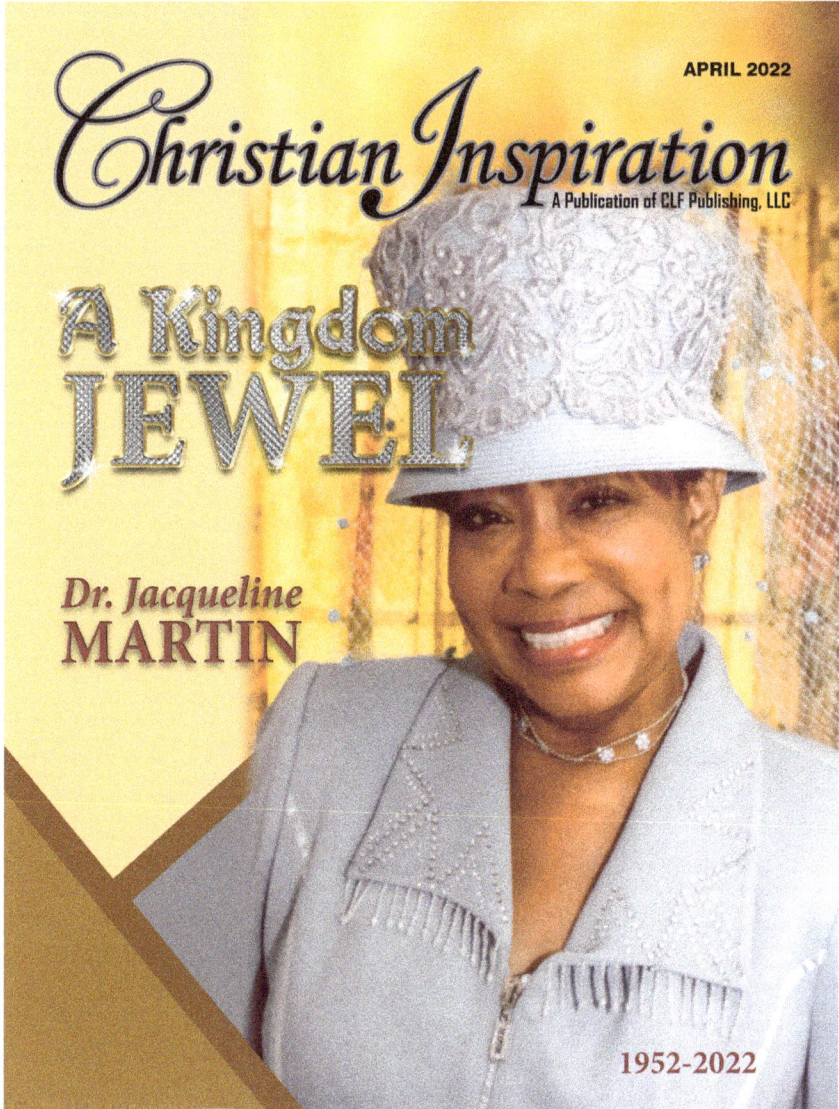

APRIL 2022

Christian Inspiration
A Publication of CLF Publishing, LLC

A Kingdom JEWEL

Dr. Jacqueline MARTIN

1952-2022

Christian Inspiration is a quarterly magazine with issues released each year in January, April, July, and October. The magazine covers topics germane to Christian living and the world at large.

DR. CASSUNDRA WHITE-ELLIOTT

THE LAST
SHALL BE
FIRST

AN ANALYSIS OF THE
SYSTEMIC SUBDIVIDE
OF BLACK AMERICA

Beginning in the early 1500s, Africans were transported to America; however, they were not permitted to live and operate as free citizens in the new land. They were enslaved and treated as property rather than human beings. Some 500 years later, people of African descent and other Blacks have yet to realize the true meaning of freedom, equality, and liberty in America. This inequity stems from sustained and systemic racism and acts of discrimination. These abhorrent acts have consistently kept Black Americans marginalized from mainstream America, depriving them of equal access to employment, education, wealth, housing, quality health care, and safety.

The modern-day slavery experience of Africans in the 1500s and 1600s (which led to the current condition of Black Americans) was similar to that of the Israelites of the 15th century B.C. as they too were enslaved. At the moment of the Israelites' liberation from Egypt, God moved mightily in their lives by transferring the wealth (gold and silver) of Egypt to the Israelites.

In this season, God desires to move mightily in the lives of Black Americans as He did for the Israelites. And, just as He did for them, He wants to complete the wealth transfer that has already been initiated, for the Bible says in Proverbs 13:22b, "…*and the wealth of the sinner is laid up for the just.*"

So, what must you do to prepare for a mighty move of God?
How can you be an agent of change?

CLF Publishing, LLC.
www.clfpublishing.org

ISBN 978-1-945102-62-2
90000

9 781945 102622

Dr. Cassundra White-Elliott's books are available at:
www.creativemindsbookstore.com
www.amazon.com
www.barnesandnoble.com

Rest in HIM

Scriptures for Daily Peace

Dr. C. White-Elliott

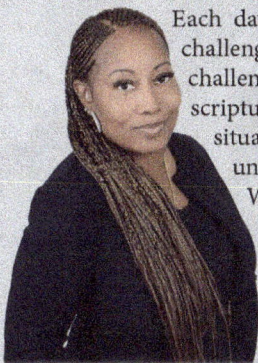

Each day brings about its own unique challenges. Yet, in the midst of the challenge you are enduring, there are scriptures that are applicable to your situation that will provide insight, understanding, and comfort. God's Word serves as our guide and provides peace in the midst of a trial or daily circumstance. The Word of God keeps us healthy and whole when we read it, meditate on it, and apply it.

Rest in Him provides Bible verses at your fingertips for easy use. Keep this handy tool close by, so you can remind yourself that the Lord is an ever-present help in the time of need.

CLF Publishing, LLC.
www.clfpublishing.org

ISBN 978-1-945102-68-4

90000

9 781945 102684

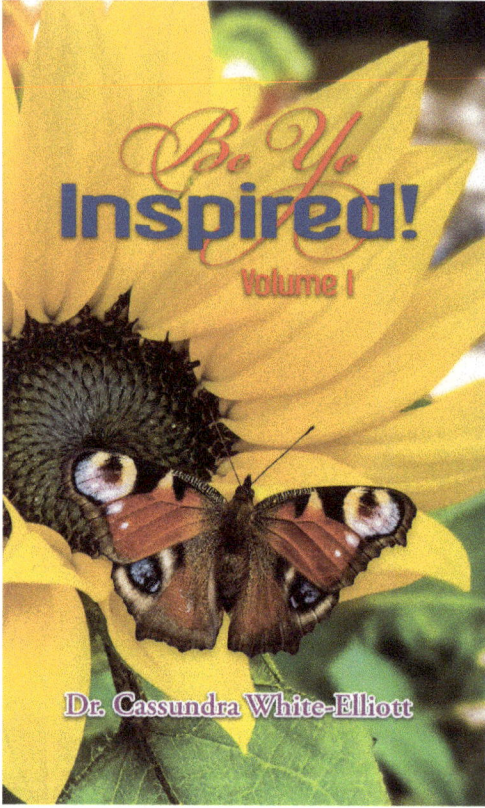

Be Ye Inspired!
Volume I

Dr. Cassundra White-Elliott

Be Ye Inspired!
Volume II

Dr. C.

www.ingramcontent.com/pod-product-compliance
Lightning Source LLC
Chambersburg PA
CBHW050014090426
42734CB00020B/3264